Blessings!
Bola Adeyofa
4/29/21

INSPIRATIONS

Two

INSPIRATIONS

Two

Bola Adepoju

INSPIRATIONS II

For copies, please visit:www.womanonpurpose.org or your online book store.

Published by:
Woman on Purpose
P.O. Box 2910
Stockbridge, Ga.30281
e-mail: pastorbola@womanonpurpose.org

Cover Art by: John Afon

Unless otherwise indicated, all Scripture quotations are from the NEW KING JAMES VERSION of the Bible.

Printed in the United States of America

TABLE OF CONTENTS

Inspirational Quotes I

Prophetic Blessings I

Inspirational Quotes II

Prophetic Blessings II

Prophetic Blessings III

DEDICATION

This book is dedicated to God my Father, to the Son my Redeemer and Savior and to the Holy Spirit my Inspiration.

ACKNOWLEDGMENTS

My special thanks to my wonderful husband and best friend, Dr. Olatunde Adepoju, who has loved, and supported me for over thirty years. Dear, you are the wind beneath my wings. I cherish your wisdom. You have been an encouragement to me in life and ministry. I love you from the depth of my heart. To my children, Timi and Dami, I thank God for giving you both to us as gifts; you are my joy. I love you very much and I'm proud of you both. To my parents, Chief and Chief (Mrs.) Emiola Adesina, who loved, nurtured me and instilled good values in me in my early years. I love you both.

My appreciation goes to Ronnie Wells for packaging this book for publishing. May you never lack help. To Darryl Peek and Dr. Cheryl Walker for your comments about the book. Your words are very inspiring. To Reverend Segun and Pastor Yemisi Adebowale, I cherish you both. Thank you for your love, over 25 years of friendship and spiritual guidance. I want to thank you so much, Pastor Roland Lane, Jr. for the task of reading the manuscript and writing the foreword. You have been a support and an encouragement to me.

Finally, to my readers, team and ministry partners, your gifts and encouraging words have kept me going and helped me to continue with the work God has called me to do. May the Lord bless you. May the Holy Spirit be your inspiration.

FOREWORD

God could not have blessed me with a more passionate and effective "sister in the ministry" than Pastor Bola Adepoju. I first met Pastor Bola in the workplace and we quickly became friends. She ministered to me every morning with prayers and devotionals that we called "morning glory." She even began to speak prophetically into my life with pinpoint accuracy and miraculous timing. Soon our relationship grew into the area of ministry partners.

Once I met her husband, Dr. Olatunde Adepoju, I fell in love with the couple. Dr. Adepoju is a powerful man of God, scholar and teacher in his own right and has not only become my mentor and friend, but also serves as one of my spiritual overseers and point of reference in my Christian walk and pastoral calling. He is truly a pastor's pastor. Together, Dr. Adepoju and Pastor Bola create a dynamic ministry team and a force to reckon with in God's kingdom. They both have a servant's heart for ministering to the least, lost and left out.

I pastor an up and coming church plant in Atlanta. My church decided to team up with Pastor Bola's outreach arm of her Woman on Purpose ministry, Project R.E.A.C.H: Restoring and Empowering a Community's Hope. We have, on many occasions, experienced miracles during these outreach efforts that only God himself could have manifested and I am so humbled by each opportunity to serve with her and be a partaker of God's favor over her life. The inexplicable numbers that we have served with so few people made me realize that we don't have to be a "mega church" to be a mega ministry if God is on our side. This, for me, was sufficient evidence of Pastor Bola's favor with God and true prophetic and ministerial anointing.

I experienced an even deeper revelation of her Spirit-filled ministry gifts when I asked her to pray for my wife who was suffering from a debilitating illness. Although my wife is a minister and anointed worshipper and prayer warrior, she was weary beyond measure by this attack from the enemy. I had even begun to question God, myself, on why this was happening to my wife. Pastor Bola noticed my uncharacteristically despondent countenance and said, "Your wife shall be healed in Jesus' name." She called my wife on the phone and went forth in prayer, speaking in God's heavenly language and boldly decreeing healing in the name of Jesus. My wife was healed of that malady the same hour and our marriage has since returned to a blissful state. I am forever grateful to God for that testimony and for sending Pastor Bola in my life to be an intercessor, encourager, prophetess and ministry partner.

This book is a revelatory and devotional masterpiece with many prophetic blessings, practical prayer points and keen, relevant applications of scripture that can only be summed up as a powerful and inspiring Word from God. If you read the pages of this book, there is no doubt that your life will be impacted, your spiritual walk enacted and your relationship with Christ transacted. The lessons and spiritual insights from this book have inspired sermons and personal growth and strength for me. It is my prayer that you and countless others seeking to hear from God's heart are similarly blessed by this transforming and practical message of Christ.

May God bless you richly and honor your faithfulness in this Christian way. Glory be to God for what He has done through Pastor Bola and this book, Inspirations II.

Roland Lane, Jr.
Lead Pastor, Harmony Church
Atlanta, Georgia

PREFACE

Before you are a collection of inspirations God laid on my heart, and I have put them together to bless you. No matter what you are going through, the promises in the Word of God, the prophetic blessings, and promises in this book will bless you and take you from where you are to where God wants you to be. It does not matter when you pick up this book, it may be 20, 30 or more years from now, it will work for you. The messages will be relevant to your situation and it will become a "now" word for you. As they have blessed, inspired, healed and encouraged many, they will do the same for you. Contrary to what one may think, this book is not for women only; it is for men and women of all ages, races and ethnic backgrounds. Many testimonies have come as a result of these words, and I believe the Holy Spirit will minister to you and cause your spirit to be lifted up. I pray as you spend time meditating on these inspirations, He will re-ignite your relationship with God the Father, Son and Holy Spirit; and each word will meet you at the point of your need. Allow God's Word in your heart and I promise it will bring transformation, reformation and definitely, restoration. This book is not really a devotional, but you can use it as one. The Prayer Focus sections will help you to pray specifically in the area of the readings that God's Word has found relevance with your own situation. They will also lead you to pray more effective prayers that the Holy Spirit will minister to your heart.

To receive the full benefit of this book, you must enter the heavenly race. In any given race, there are rules to follow. Many people lose in the race because they do not follow the rules. The Number One rule in our heavenly race is that your name must be recorded in the Lamb's book of life. To enter the race, you must be born again. If you are not sure you are born again, please take the time to settle that issue now by making your way to the section in this book on, "Whose Guest Will I be At the End?", and saying the prayer first. After doing that, all the blessings written in this book and in the Word of God automatically will become yours. Read each article carefully and allow the Holy Spirit to speak to you. As He speaks to you, do whatever He says you should do. Applying the Word of God in this book will give you wisdom. It will make you a winner and a champion. It will cause you to soar like an eagle. Do not give up. Do not give in. Stay strong and focus on God. Make a determination to finish your race well. It is up to you!!!!

1

It is a Fresh Start!!!

In December 1914, spontaneous combustion broke out in Thomas Edison's, the inventor of the light bulbs, film room laboratory. Within minutes, his life's work was in flames! Fire companies from eight surrounding cities arrived, but the heat was so intense and the water pressure so low that the attempt to douse the flames was futile. Everything was destroyed! Edison was 67 years old. With all his assets estimated at over two million dollars in flames, the buildings were only insured for only $238,000. Was his spirit broken? Did he give up? No!! While his 24 year old son, Charles cried at the loss, Thomas said, "Where is your mother? Find her. Bring her here. She will never see anything like this as long as she lives." Edison looked at the ruins and said, "There is great value in disaster. All our mistakes are burned up. Thank God we can start anew." He saw it as an opportunity for a fresh start.

Have you lost something of value and have given up trying again? Or have you wasted time in the past years making a list of unfulfilled goals? Like Edison, you can start all over. It does not matter where you are right now, you can still make a fresh start. You can begin to write down your goals and make a decision to put the goals into actions. You can pick up the pieces and start afresh. However, if you have not started

Prayer Focus

- Repent for allowing life, situations, circumstances, and people to cause you not to follow up with the goals you have set out to do every year.

- Ask the Lord to begin to open your heart to all that He wants you to do.

- Ask the Lord to give you a fresh start; the grace to begin to write something glorious in your "life book."

- Ask the Lord to redeem your time and to restore every year that you have lost.

- Ask that as you go on this new journey, the Holy Spirit will go with you and prosper your way.

to put your goals into actions, you have another opportunity for a fresh start. It is not too late. As the saying goes, "It is better late than never." The Lord has given you another opportunity for life to start afresh. He has given you a blank sheet of paper to begin to write something in it. Each minute, hour, day, week and month is a precious gift He has given to you so that you can begin to write in the book that will make up history for you. Just as Edison made history, so can you.

It is a time of a fresh word, fresh anointing, fresh insight, fresh new ideas, fresh territory to conquer, fresh grace, and fresh zeal. He says it does not matter how you got to where you are or what you did in the past; you can still make it. He has given you another opportunity to write in your "Life book". It does not matter what happened in the past, whether it was due to your fault or not, you must be determined in your heart right now not to give up, not to spend your God-given time wastefully or waste your God-given resources. Your life must have a purpose. You must be answer-minded not problem-minded. There are projects and ideas that you shelved in the past years; pick them up. There are things you think you cannot do; "Receive the Boost" by the power of the Holy Ghost!!! Paul said, "I can do all things through Christ, (the Anointed One and His Anointing) which strengthens me." (Philippians 4:13). This verse is not a slogan, but a reality in the life of Thomas Edison. If it worked for Edison, it will surely work for you. Believe it will, and it will. Religion

Prayer Focus

- ◆ Declare that nothing will stop the move of God in your life.
- ◆ Declare that you will not die until you do all God has apportioned for you on this side of eternity.
- ◆ Declare that you will experience God's presence in a fresh way every day of your life.
- ◆ Declare that your life will not be a waste.

Begin to declare the following in the name of Jesus: My past will no longer hold me bound. My past will not limit my future. My future is glorious. My shame is over. I roll away every stone of reproach and shame in my life. I am blessed in my generation. Because of me generations after me will suffer no more. Where others in my family have failed, I will succeed. I am not a quitter. I am a savior in my family. Generations after me will call me blessed. The joy of the Lord is my strength.

Prayer Focus

- Declare that the anointing of the Holy Ghost will break the hold of stagnancy and mediocrity over your life.

- Ask the Lord to turn every loss into an opportunity for a breakthrough.

- Ask Him to give you the grace not to give up no matter what is happening or what has happened in your life.

- Pray that the Lord will cause your losses and mistakes to become opportunities for greatness.

- Declare that the enemy will not have the last word over your life, family and destiny.

may try to rob you of the blessings in the Word. Situations, circumstances, friends and even family members may try to talk you out of them, stand on your Word and it will work for you. Command your soul not to be cast down. A crisis in your life can be God's voice speaking to you. It can be God's way of saying, "A new agenda is about to emerge or a new door is about to open." There is the Anointing of the Anointed One which is present in you to enable you do exploits for God. He is present to move you to your next level; to help you in areas of your weaknesses; to move you from mediocrity to excellence; and from being oppressed to being the oppressor. He moves you from being sick to being healed. It is not by power or by might, but by His Spirit (Zachariah 4:6).

Make short term goals that will lead you to long term goals. Do not weigh yourself down with unrealistic goals. Take the first step and begin to climb your mountain. You do not have to be like everybody else. God has deposited in you unique gifts and abilities that will enable you to accomplish whatever He needs for you to do. You are not a failure going somewhere to happen, but you are a success going somewhere to be expressed. You are blessed of the Lord and you will fulfill destiny. You are not a waste. You are a uniquely packaged gift of God to that school, home, church, work place or community. Take that step of faith. Conquer new grounds; write that book; start that business. Make plans to get rid of your debt. Go to school. Do something. You do not have time to waste. Time is running out and it will not wait for you.

The Lord will begin to do exceeding abundantly above all that you ask or think according to His power that lives in you!! Begin to write in your "Life book". You are off to a new beginning; a fresh start. You will make it. You have started well, and you will complete it well. Join me as we cross over to the other side!!!

Reference Scripture

"Behold, I will do a new thing; now it shall spring forth; shall ye not know it? I will even make a way in the wilderness, and rivers in the desert." – Isaiah 43:19

2

Replaced or a Replacement?

"So Samuel took the horn of oil and anointed him in the presence of his brothers, and from that day on the Spirit of the LORD came upon David in power. Now the Spirit of the LORD had departed from Saul, and an evil spirit from the LORD tormented him." I Samuel 16:13-14

Have you ever wondered how an anointed person can lose his anointing, lose his relevance and all of a sudden be replaced by another? This is what happened to King Saul. God had a plan and purpose for Saul. Saul started well, but he did not end well. When he messed up and disobeyed God, he was replaced by David. As David was being anointed king in his stead, God's Spirit rested on David. At the same time, an evil spirit rested on Saul. There was not only a physical replacement, there was a spiritual one! What a shame!

Prayer Focus

♦ Plead the blood of Jesus on yourself and declare that your mistakes will not become a curse in the lives of your children and their children.

♦ Instead of being replaced, ask the Lord to make you a replacement. Ask Him to make you an Esther, David, or a Mathias in your generation.

The same thing happened to Eli the priest. When he started messing up and was unable to control his sons who were doing abominable things in the house of God, God prepared Samuel as a replacement. In I Samuel 1:35, God told Eli that He would raise a faithful priest to replace him. When Judas betrayed Jesus, he was replaced by Mathias. How about Esther replacing Vashti? Have you been replaced or are you a replacement? Are you running God's agenda or your agenda? It is not too late to get back on track. God has not and will not give up on you.

If God has given you an assignment, you cannot afford to fail him. If you do, He will prepare a replacement or a substitute for the same assignment. You are on an

Prayer Focus

- Ask the Lord for strength to rise from your ashes.
- Ask the Lord to give you the grace to end well. If you have not started at all, ask Him to lead you so you can begin and end well.
- The blessings of the Lord makes rich and adds no sorrows. Ask the Lord not to cause His blessings in your life to become your down fall.
- Receive grace and anointing to begin to live for things greater than you.
- Receive everything you need spiritually, physically, emotionally, materially and financially to fulfill your purpose.

assignment in your home, church, workplace, business, subdivision, community, state and country.

God did not choose you because you are the best candidate or the best qualified; He chose you because He called and picked you out. God does not call the qualified; He qualifies the called. So you cannot take His grace for granted. You must remember that you are not indispensable, but you can be and are replaceable. You must count yourself privileged to be called and used by Him.

Saul's children could have reigned over Israel. Jesus Christ could have come from his lineage, but He came from David's. The priesthood could have remained in Eli's family, but he was cut off. Whatever you do or do not do can affect generations after you. Your assignment is not only for your benefit, it is for the benefit of generations after you. There are destinies connected to yours. You must always bear in mind that you are living for something greater than you. You are anointed for greatness. God is increasing your potential. He is establishing you. He says you can do it. Be ready, be available, be obedient and be faithful. Go in His strength and His power will sustain you. Know that He who has called you will not leave or forsake you. He has your back. You will not be replaced spiritually

When God gives you an assignment, do not fail him. If you do, He will prepare a replacement or a substitute for the same assignment. You are on that assignment in your home, church, workplace....., not because you are the best candidate or the best qualified, but because God called and chose you for it.

or physically in Jesus' name. You will not be displaced or replaced in your home, church, office, business or ministry.

You are an important part of God's program. You are on an assignment. Stay focused. Stay on target. Be steadfast, unshakeable, and immovable and you will fulfill your destiny!

Scripture Reference
"They shall not build, and another inhabit; they shall not plant, and another eat: for as the days of a tree, so shall be the days of my people, and my elect shall long enjoy the work of their hands. They shall not labor in vain, nor bring forth for trouble......" Isaiah 65:22-23

3

If I be…..Then Let Fire Fall!

II Kings 1:1-13

Ahaziah, King of Samaria, fell off the balcony rail of his house and became sick. He sent messengers to consult Baal-Zebub, the god of Ekron to inquire if he would recover from his sickness. The angel of the Lord told Elijah to intercept the messengers and give them a word from the Lord for the King, "*Is it because there is no God in Israel that you are going to inquire of Baal-Zebub, the god of Ekron?" Now therefore, thus says the Lord: 'You shall not come down from the bed to which you have gone up, but you shall surely die'* (*I Kings 1:3-4*). So the messengers returned to the king with the word from the man of God. When the messengers gave the king this word, he wanted to know who had the nerve to give him such a report. His messengers described the man to him, and the king immediately knew who it was. It was Elijah!!! So he sent one of the captains of his army and fifty soldiers with him to go and bring Elijah to him. Elijah said, "*If I am a man of God, then let fire come down from heaven and consume you and your fifty men.*" And fire came down from heaven and consumed the captain of the army and his fifty soldiers. Again Ahaziah sent another captain and his fifty men to get Elijah. Elijah said again, "*If I am a man of God, then let fire come down from heaven and consume you and your fifty men.*" Again fire came down and consumed them. The king sent another captain and his fifty, and this time the captain, who had seen others destroyed at Elijah's command fell down at Elijah's feet

> Do you not wonder why the king had to send fifty-one men to bring in one man? I do. The answer is simple. He knew what he was up against. He knew Elijah's reputation as a man of God; he was a fighter. He knew him as the prophet that killed 450 prophets of Baal in I Kings 18. He knew Elijah had spiritual authority and backing. He was no joke. What does the enemy know about you?

Does he think you are a push over or does he recognize that you know your rights as a child of God? Does he tremble when you speak or do you tremble when he speaks? Are you the predator or the prey?

You are a battle axe; a caterpillar, a bulldozer, a destructive force against the kingdom of darkness. Do you know it?

to beg for his life, and the life of his men. Are you scared of your adversary or is he scared of you? Is he terrorizing you or have you been terrorizing him?

Do you not wonder why the king had to send fifty men to bring in one man? I do. The answer is simple. He knew what he was up against. He knew Elijah's reputation as a man of God; he was a fighter; a warrior. He was a force to reckon with. He knew him as the prophet who challenged and killed 450 prophets of Baal in I Kings 18. He knew Elijah had spiritual

authority and backing. He was no joke. He was not a push over. He knew the God Elijah served was a consuming fire.

What does the enemy know about you? Does he think you are a push over or does he recognize that you know your rights as a child of God? Does he tremble when you speak or does the reverse occur? Are you the predator or the prey? Elijah said to those men confidently, "If I am a man of God......." He was the challenger. He knew his right. He was sure of his identity. He knew his words were not ordinary words. Fire fell at his words. They had the backing of God's power and anointing. Fire must fall at your words. The kingdom of the enemy must tremble at your words. You are empowered to devastate the kingdom of darkness. You are a battle axe; a caterpillar, a bulldozer and a destructive force against the kingdom of darkness. Do you know it? Do

Prayer Focus

♦ Command God's fire to fall upon your tongue and ask heaven to back up every word you pronounce against the kingdom of darkness.

♦ Ask the heavens to back up every word of blessing that proceeds out of your mouth.

♦ Declare that at your word the kingdom of darkness will fall.

♦ Ask the Lord to seal every edge that is broken or anything that the enemy can use against you with the blood of Jesus.

♦ Receive grace to speak God's truth no matter the cost.

Prayer Focus

♦ Declare that the fire of God will fall on you to re-ignite you spiritually.

♦ Just as the Lord made a spectacle of the Prophets of Baal, ask Him to make a spectacle of everything that has defeated, challenged or embarrassed you in the past.

♦ There are people who have to believe that there is a God in heaven just by what is happening in your life. Ask God to cause your testimonies to bring many to the saving knowledge of our Lord Jesus.

you enforce it? Does the enemy recognize it? The devil will try to get you just as he tried to get Elijah. You must let him know who's boss, you!!! The devil did not try him once; he did it three times and Elijah kept on destroying them and showing them that they had no power over him. You cannot afford to give up even when he strikes more than once. You must keep on getting up and firing at him in Jesus' name!!! Greater is He that is in you (I John 4:4). The devil must and will fall at your feet. You cannot and must not allow him to take you, or your children, or your spouse or your home, or your mind, or your health or anything that is dear to you. You must cause "your fire" to fall in Jesus' name. Isaiah 54:17 says, *"No weapon formed against you shall prosper, and every tongue which rises against you in judgment you shall condemn.* **This is the heritage of the servants of the Lord....."** *It* is your right as a child of God.

Can you speak the truth no matter what it is going to cost you? Are you feared by the adversary or do you fear you him? Do you know who you are in God? Can you confidently say like Elijah, "If I am, then.......let....?"

This season two types of fire will fall; one on you and the other on your adversary. The first fire is the type that fell on the disciples on the day of Pentecost. This fire re-fueled re-ignited and empowered and defended them against every attack of the enemy. It was this fire that energized the disciples to do the work of the kingdom. It is the same fire that descended on Samson in Judges 15:14 that cause the new ropes that were used to bind him to become like flax that was burned with fire. He was unhurt. Similarly, in Daniel 3:23-25, when Shadrach, Meshach, and Abednego were hurled into Nebuchadnezzar's fiery furnace, they were unhurt because they landed into the

> **Declare the following:**
>
> I am anointed to devastate the kingdom of the enemy. Whatever I decree is established in Jesus' name. Everything the enemy throws at me is destroyed in Jesus' name. I am a fighter. Every day I wake up the kingdom of darkness is in trouble. I will not give up, give in or give out in Jesus' name.

Consuming Fire's protective arms. Meanwhile, the ropes that bound them were burned. Your assurance is that you do not have to fear when you go through fire because the Consuming Fire is with you. The Fire will protect you and consume your adversary. I command the fire of the Holy Ghost to fall afresh on you now in Jesus' name. I command the fire to purge and cleanse you so you can experience God's glory, power and anointing like you have never done before in Jesus' name. It is the fire on Elijah that caused him to become a terror to the adversary. That fire will and must fall on you in Jesus' name!!! Block any avenue that the accuser may use against you. Live right and fear the Lord.

The second fire is the one to consume every demonic activity, influence, mountain, Pharaoh, or Goliath over your life and destiny. Now, I call down fire from heaven to begin to destroy every plan of the adversary over your life, destiny, family, children, finance, marriage, finances, or health, in Jesus' name. They will come against you one way and flee seven ways (Deuteronomy 28:7). God's anointing, power and glory will separate you from the rest. The disasters that have plagued many in your family will not touch you. God's fire will begin to make you a force to reckon with spiritually. You are empowered to do exploit. You do not have the spirit of fear, but of power, of love, and a sound mind (II Timothy 1:7). Just as the captain of the third army fell down at Elijah's feet, the adversary will fall down at your feet. You are all God says you are. You are more than a conqueror in Jesus' name. **AMEN**.

Scripture Reference
"Yet in all these things we are more than conquerors through Him who loved us." - Romans 8:37.

4

Go Forward, Slack Not!!!

II Kings 4:18-36

The above mentioned passage talks about the story of the Shunammite woman whose son died. When this woman realized what had happened, she knew exactly what she had to do. Her son was a miracle from God and she knew exactly where to go for restoration. She knew time was of the essence and she had to see Elisha, the man of God and receive her miracle. So she told her husband she needed an ass and one of the servants so could make this life-saving trip without wasting any more time. Her husband knew where she was going and why she was going to see Elisha, but he did not seem to understand the urgency of her demand. The boy was already dead. Why bother the man of God? He said, Why today; why not tomorrow or the day after? It is no longer important. It is no longer urgent. The deed has already been done. Why not do it some other time? It is neither the time nor the season for miracles. What you are trying to do is strange. Why do you have to reach out for your miracle now? Wait and do it another time. It is not done this way. It is not culturally correct!!! Traditionally, it has been done another way; why change things now? You are going outside the norm. It is bound to fail if you don't do it like others have done it. It will definitely not work out. Others have done it one way and it has worked for them; why do you want to do it another way?" Her response to him was, "It is well!!!"

> You may have shared something that the Lord has laid on your heart with people and instead of them encouraging you, they say it is ridiculous. They have discouraged you and have said that it won't work or it is not the right time. Maybe it is a new idea and you know if you share it with people, it will sound ridiculous, far-fetched and unattainable. Don't worry. God says, "This season He will be using people to do things outside the norm....."

12

Prayer Focus

♦ Declare that your expectations physically, spiritually, materially and emotionally will not be cut off in Jesus' name.

♦ Receive grace to say "No" to every "nay sayer" in your life.

♦ Frustrate every spirit of tradition or "old system." Ask that the Holy Spirit will come alive in your life.

♦ Receive grace not to be easily discouraged or frustrated in Jesus' name.

♦ Declare you will not be in the dark; ask that the word of the Lord will come to you every time you need it.

You may have shared something that the Lord has laid on your heart with people and instead of them encouraging you, they tell you that your idea is ridiculous. They have discouraged you and have said that it won't work or it's not the right time. May be it is a new idea and you know if you share it with people, it will sound ridiculous, far-fetched and unattainable. Don't worry. God says, "This season He will be using people to do things outside the norm. They will do unconventional things in ministry and in business that will yield unusual results. He will use you in your office, in your home, in your community, in that political office, and in your school." Even when the Shunammite woman knew her son was dead, she did not give up. She knew what she had to do and she did not waste time doing it. It didn't matter what time of the day, month or year it was. It didn't matter what people before her did. She was not concerned about maintaining the status-quo. She did not care about being "politically correct." She saddled her ass and prepared for her journey. She embarked on the journey in spite of opposition. The Lord says, "The process will look strange not just to you, but to others, but the result will be great and rewarding. The path may also look strange, trust the PROMISE (the Word).

In verse 35, her son came back to life!!! What is that prophetic word that is stagnant in your life? What has the Lord told you to do that "nay sayers" say is impossible? What has He told you to do that you have set aside because of difficulties? What projects have you abandoned because people say the timing is not right? The Shunammite woman saddled her ass and said to her servant, "Drive, go forward, slack not your riding for me until I tell you to stop." There are many that have big projects, ministries, God-given and God-ordained visions and ideas that are on hold because of discouragers, discouragements, obstacles and difficulties. You may have put your dream on hold because it looked like everything at the time was bleak and nothing would work. God is saying, "Saddle your ass, drive, go forward, keep riding, keep doing it until I say it is

Prayer Focus

♦ Ask the Lord to give you the heart of a giver.

♦ Reject every known and unknown baggage in your life; declare everything that has not allowed you to move forward in the past be removed in Jesus' name.

♦ In Kings 4, the Shunammite woman was rewarded with a son because she sowed into the life of a man of God. Declare every seed that you have sown all your life will begin to bring great rewards.

♦ Pray that your expectations over your children will not be aborted.

♦ Pray that the Lord will send help when you need it.

♦ Pray that your visions and dreams will not be dashed by dream killers in Jesus' name.

okay to stop. I am the Alpha and Omega; Beginning and the Ending. I am the One who gave you the dream and I am the only One that can tell you it is over or when to stop. "He says, "Listen to Me; let me direct you. Let not man, situations, or detractors stop you. It is not too late to pick up where you have left off. I know you have tried to do it another way." You may be asking, "Why do I have to do it differently?" The Lord is saying, "It is because you are different. You are unique. You are a history maker. You are a pacesetter. Do not be afraid. You are the one to tell the world that I cannot and will not be put in a box. I cannot be confined by culture and tradition!!! I am Sovereign. I am the One that determines the time and the season, not man. While others are waiting for the sign of the time, you must be waiting on My Word. While others are copying and replicating old systems that are no longer working, you must be constantly asking Me; "What are you saying now; what must I do now?" I am the One saying this is your season or the unusual. It is your season to succeed where others think you will fail. It is your season to surprise your detractors, to encourage the discouraged and give hope to the hopeless. It is your season to enjoy mouth-dropping, eye-popping, ear-tingling testimonies in Jesus' name. Keep soaring eagle, do not slack. You will not fail!!"

Scripture Reference

"Being confident of this very thing, that He who has begun a good work in you will complete it until the day of Jesus Christ" – Philippians 1:6.

5

A Table Before You in Their Midst!!!

Judges 11:1-8

The above mentioned passage talks about the story of a mighty man of valor named Jephthah. However, Jephthah was born by a harlot to his father, Gilead. When His father's sons by the legitimate wife grew up and realized that he was the son of a harlot, they drove him out of his father's house. They said that they did not want him to be a partaker of their inheritance. Jephthah had no choice but to flee from them. A "man of valor" found himself in the midst of worthless men. He was no better than them because that was what his family and his country people thought he was. Then God created a situation in Israel that made the people who had cast Jephthah out to come looking for him to deliver them.

Those that drove him away now came to beg him to be their leader. Those who scorned him came begging for his help. Even though they thought he was "a nobody", God saw greatness in him. He could not be overlooked. They had to see what God saw in him. He was a leader and he was going to be their leader! What an awesome God! They realized that he was a man of valor. He had what it took to rescue Israel from the hands of her adversaries! They knew he had what it

Prayer Focus

- ♦ Ask the Lord to remove every stigma from your past that the enemy is using to haunt you.
- ♦ Ask the Lord to make you a show piece in your family, work place, church and community.
- ♦ Ask Him to create situations that will make your detractors seek your help.

Prayer Focus

- ♦ Receive grace to forgive those who have slandered your name or have hurt you in any way. Ask the Lord to purge you of unforgiveness and bitterness in your heart.
- ♦ Receive grace to forge ahead in spite of limitations.

15

took to lead their nation to war and win!!! He was a force that could not be ignored. Even though they thought he was worthless, God had to prove them wrong. Even though they ostracized him for something he had no control over, God made him relevant in the history of a nation. His past was irrelevant because God brought him from the midst of worthlessness to become a leader of his people. God made him a showpiece not only before the brothers that rejected him, but before all of Israel. It is amazing how God can use the foolish things of this world to confound the wise!

> .... God created a situation in Israel that made the people who had cast Jephthah out to come looking for him to deliver them.
>
> Those that drove him away now came to beg him to be their leader. Even though they thought he was a "nobody", God saw greatness in him; he could not be overlooked. They could not but see the leader in him. God created a situation to make those that had scorned him to come begging for his help. What an awesome God!!! He was a man of valor. He had what it took to rescue Israel from the hands of her adversaries. He had what it took to lead a whole nation to war and win!!! He was a force to reckon with. Even though they thought he was worthless, God had to prove them wrong.

What in your past or present is the devil using to haunt you? It does not matter whether or not you were or are the cause of it. God is merciful to deliver you from every scorn of the enemy. What does the enemy keep reminding you of that wants to make you think that you cannot be used by God in that church or ministry, in that business, workplace or family? What does he constantly remind you of that makes you think you are not worthy or that there are others better that can do the job? What is he using to steal your self-esteem? What is he doing that is making you think that there are others better than you that can make the difference? Even if your family or those who are close to you have written you off, God is saying, "I have not written you off. I am opening a book of remembrance for you. I am causing those who have slandered your name to come seeking your forgiveness and your help. I am doing a new thing in your life and family. I am causing you to forget your wounds because I am healing them. *Do not remember the former things, nor consider the things of old. Behold, I will do a new thing, now it shall spring forth; shall you not know it? I will even make a road in the wilderness and rivers in the desert*" (Isaiah 43:18-19). He is also saying, "Forgive all those who have hurt you. Forgive all that have done you wrong." A whole nation was saved because of a forgiving man. He will set a table before you in the presence of your enemies. He will make a way for you in your wilderness and will bring water from your dry places. He will make things easy for you. Your past will no longer be a limitation or barrier to you. He is also saying, "Your case may be like Jephthah; your parents may have given you your DNA, but I am giving you a new birth and a new beginning. My blood is cleansing you right now from your past and giving you a new DNA. You must not allow your past to become your prison. You have a say in your life; you have a voice in your destiny. You have a choice in the path you take. Even though you have met with stumbling blocks, I will make a way for you. You will be relevant in the destiny of your detractors. Whatever or whoever caused you to flee or be ashamed in the past will run after you to seek your favor. You will no longer be overlooked. There is more ahead of you than behind you. I promise you beauty for your ashes; the oil of joy for your mourning, the garment of praise for the spirit of heaviness."

Scripture Reference
"You prepare a table before me in the presence of my enemies: you anoint my head with oil; my cup runs over." - Psalm 23:5.

17

Inspirational Quotes

1

◈ "One day you might see yourself walking alone on a new path. No one seems in sight. No one seems to have walked it earlier. Don't give up midway. You are on a right track. Go on; fulfill your dreams. Reach your goal. The reason why you do not see anyone is because the world is following you!" - Anonymous

◈ "Knowledge is not power; knowledge that you apply becomes power in your life." - Anonymous

◈ "You don't change people's mind by the words you speak, but you inspire change in their hearts by the life you live." - Anonymous

◈ "If you don't have the courage to walk alone, others will not have the courage to walk with you."-Anonymous

◈ "Strong people stand for themselves, but stronger people stand for others." - Anonymous

◈ "You can see great things from the valley; but only small things from the peak." -Gilbert K. Chesterton

◈ "Since most of us spend our lives doing ordinary tasks, the most important thing is to carry them out extraordinarily well." - Henry David Thoreau

◈ "We make a living by what we get, but we make a life by what we give." - Winston Churchill

◈ "A bend in your road of life is not the end of the road for you, unless you refuse to make that next turn." – Anonymous

◆ "The manifestation of your dream is not guaranteed until you decide to work it out or fight it out."–Anonymous

◆ "A hero and a coward are both confronted with fear. The only difference is that the hero confronts the fear and transforms it into fire."- Anonymous

◆ "It may last for a minute, or an hour, or a day, or a year, but it will eventually subside. If you quit, however, it will last forever." - Lance Armstrong

◆ "You block your dreams when you allow your fear to grow bigger than your faith." - Mary Morrissey

◆ "A wise man in a storm prays to God not for safety from danger, but from deliverance from fear." – Anonymous

◆ "Vision is not seeing things as they are, but as they will be." – Anonymous

6

God's Mercy at Work

Abraham was an idol worshiper who lived in the midst of idol worshipers. There was nothing about his life or his lineage that warranted God's mercy and favor. In Genesis 11:31, Abraham's father, Terah, left his people to go to the Promised Land. He did not make it because he got to Haran, lived and died there!!! God picked Abraham out and said he would not fail like his father. God made sure that his destiny was not truncated by death and that he did not make the place of transition (Haran) his final destination. God took him out from his people and took him to a place no one in his family had ever been. He gave him a blessing no one in his family had ever possessed. He was not only blessed; generations after him are blessed!!! Why? It was because of God's mercy and compassion.

David, too, was slaving away in the backside of the mountain unaware of the destiny-changing event that was taking place in his home. He was not supposed to be part of that event because he was not invited to it. However, God's mercy singled him out to favor him in the midst of his brethren. Esther the orphan slave was no material for the throne, but God vacated the throne so that a destiny that should have been forgotten would be revisited and restored. Why? It was because of God's mercy and compassion. God's mercy will create vacancies for His favor for you. God will move

> Abraham was an idol worshiper, who lived in the midst of idol worshipers. There was nothing about his life or his lineage that warranted God's mercy and favor.... God picked Abraham out and said he would not fail like his father.
>
> David too was slaving away in the backside of the mountain unaware of the destiny-changing event that was taking place in his home. He was not supposed to be part of that event because he was not invited to it. However, God's mercy singled him out for His favor in the midst of his brethren.

Prayer Focus

◆ Ask Him to make you an example in your home, family, school, work place, church and community others want to emulate.

◆ Ask Him to revisit your life and make you a part of destiny-changing events.

◆ Ask that the Lord's mercy and compassion will take you to heights no one in your family, in your business industry and in your work place has attained.

◆ Ask Him to give you grace to fill the vacancies He has opened for you and to fill positions you are not qualified for.

you to a place of power and prominence in your family, in your workplace, in your ministry, in your school and everywhere you go in the mighty name of Jesus.

It will be so evident that it could not have been anything or anyone but God. He will move you to that place not because you have merited it or because you are qualified, but because of His mercy. I see a lot of vacancies opening up for people to occupy spiritually and economically. There will be vacancies for scholarships, for promotions in offices and promotions in ministry. I see many replacing those who have occupied positions because they have become redundant, unneeded and irrelevant in God's end-time program. Many will have to vacate because they have been disobedient to God and have done their own thing. That will not be your portion in Jesus' name. There are some Davids emerging to take the place of their Sauls; Esthers emerging to take the place of their Vashtis and Mathiases emerging to take the place of their Judases. Why? God's mercy is creating vacancies for the ones that have been forgotten. He has marked you out and says you are next in line!!! God's mercy will single you out for His favor. His mercy will prevail over your life, family and situation. The anointing for favor will rest upon you. All you have been denied before now will be given to you. All you have struggled for in the past will no longer be a struggle. They will come to you easily and effortlessly. Your debts will be forgiven. Court cases will be dismissed. People who know you will favor you. People who do not know you will favor you. People who like you will favor you. People who do not like you will favor you. People will go out of their way to

God's mercy will create vacancies for His favor for you. God will move you to a place of power and prominence ....and everywhere you go in the mighty name of Jesus. It will be so evident that it could not have been anything or anyone but God.

- Receive grace to be relevant in the Lord's end-time program.

- Ask that the Lord's favor will rest upon you and take you to places no one in your family has been; cause you to see things no one in your family has seen.

please you. You will become impossible to by-pass. In Exodus 12:13, the mark of God's favor was upon the Israelites while the Egyptians were been marked for destruction. God's mark will rest upon you and your family. Every job, promotion and blessing that belongs to you that have been taken will be restored in the mighty name of Jesus. The favor you will experience will open more doors of favor. Your favor will attract more favor. You favor will be contagious. Your generation will be blessed by God's favor on your life. You will not fail like your predecessors in Jesus' name. Amen!!! When things begin to happen, acknowledge the Giver of the blessings. Stay humble. Remember, God resists the proud. If you are not humble, you might also be replaced. Do not forget to give God all the glory!! This is a word of caution.

Reference Scripture

"For You, O LORD, will bless the righteous; With favor You will surround him as *with* a shield." -**Psalm 5:12**

7

And Ye Shall Live and Know....

Ezekiel 37:1-14

This passage talks about the Spirit of the Lord taking Prophet Ezekiel to a valley full of dry bones. These bones were bones of men who had been slain in battle. The Bible says that the bones were very dry and I am assuming that the people had been dead a very long time. When Ezekiel inspected the bones, I am sure that he knew that there was no hope for these people who had been dead and forgotten, except by divine intervention. So when God asked him, "Can these bones live?" His response was, "O Lord, You know." He knew that life, physically and naturally, could not come into this valley unless God said it. When God told him to prophesy to the dry bones, he did so quickly. God was saying, "These bones will live again." Although their destiny had been aborted, He still had an assignment for them. Their destiny was not concluded and it was not yet over for them. He was giving them another chance to live and fulfill destiny. God's breath was going to revive them again!!!

> Although their destiny had been aborted, He still had an assignment for them; their destiny was not concluded and it was not over for them yet. He was giving them another chance to live and fulfill destiny. God's breath was going to revive them again!!!
>
> God is empowering you to prophesy upon anything that is dead, dying, unfruitful and barren in your life today. God is saying, "I will heal you; speak life and healing to your body. You will not die now even if the

Are you experiencing the valley of dry bones? Is your body dying and there does not seem to be anything the doctors can do to restore it? Is your son or daughter going astray and there doesn't seem to be anything you can do about it? Speak to your dry bones, and it shall live again. You shall know that the Lord is your God!!! God is empowering you to prophesy upon anything that is dead, dying, unfruitful and barren in your life today. God is saying, "I will heal you; speak life and healing to your body.

You will not die now even if the devil has a death sentence on your life!!! Just as I attached tendons, and covered the skeletons with flesh and skin, I will cover your nakedness and I will cover your shame with my glory. I will put life into everything that is dead or dying in your life. You will live to declare my glory. I will give you beauty for your ashes and the oil of joy for your mourning. You are not on your way to hell. Your child on drugs or in trouble is not on the way to hell. Your siblings or parents that do not know Me are not on the way to hell. They will receive My life, become My children and enjoy everlasting life. I will put my glory on you and you shall know that I am your God."

It was not only the dry bones that knew that God is Lord. Everyone that saw this miracle happen in their lives knew it. I prophesy upon you today, "You will become a show piece for all that know you. God will transform your life spiritually, physically, academically, materially and financially. As there was a shaking that put the bones together, I declare that the Lord will shake off shame and reproach from your life. He will put order back into your life. You shall become fruitful again. You shall live again. You will begin to operate spiritually at a level you have never operated before, and you will do what you have never done before. Your latter end will be greater than your former. The Lord will restore every abandoned project in your life. The life the enemy and sickness stole from you is restored as from today in Jesus' name. The child the enemy stole to drugs is restored in Jesus' name. I prophesy to you barren, bear fruit. I prophesy to you hopeless, receive hope. If you have been uncovered receive divine cover and receive beauty and honor. If you are lost, receive

> **Prayer Focus**
> - Plead the blood of Jesus over every organ, tissue, vein, or muscle that is dying in your life.
> - Ask the Lord to anoint your tongue as you begin to prophesy upon your life, body, family, business, church, ministry, community and to nations.
> - Command the power that raised Jesus up from the dead to breathe life into everything that is dead or dying in your life and family.
> - Command every good thing that is on life support in your life to be resuscitated today in Jesus' name.
> - Just as the Lord covered the dry bones with flesh and life, ask the Lord to cover your nakedness with His glory.

direction. If you have been afflicted and oppressed receive deliverance today. I go to the root of every sickness in your body and family and curse them in the name of Jesus."

If dry bones could hear the Word of the Lord and respond, no matter how bad your situation is, it will hear God's voice today and respond in Jesus' name. Death will recognize your voice and respond with life. The enemy will recognize your voice and respond. Sorrow will hear your voice today and flee. God is breathing upon you, upon your family, upon your children and upon your situation no matter how difficult it is. I prophesy upon the four winds of the Earth to breathe, breathe and breathe in Jesus' name. **AMEN**.

Reference Scripture

"But as it is written, eye hath not seen, nor ear heard, neither have entered into the heart of man, the things which God hath prepared for them that love him" – I Corinthians 2:9.

8

Too Hot to Handle!

Acts 12:1-18

When God says that your season of release and your time to break loose has come, no demon from the pit of hell can stop it. This was Peter's case. Herod took and killed James, John's brother. When he saw that it pleased the Jews, he decided to take Peter also. He bound Peter and put him in prison. On the night before Peter's trial, the angel of the Lord appeared to him, woke him up and told him to get up. As soon as Peter got up, the chains that bound him were loosed and he was free. The angel led him to the city gates, and the gates opened unto Peter on their own accord. What a powerful testimony!!! The enemy that has been fooling with your life and destiny must be stopped. The enemy that says you will die before your time must be stopped. The enemy that says many will weep and mourn over you and your family must be stopped. Your troubler must stop. He must be put to shame. Herod had been troubling the Christians in the Church and persecuting them; but there was no one to stop him until he took the wrong person. You will become too hot for the adversary to handle. Herod thought that he would succeed taking and killing Peter just as he succeeded in taking and killing James. The Lord said it was not Peter's time. The Lord that said it was not Peter's time is saying that it is not yet your time. It is not your time to die. You will not be defeated. You will not be put to shame. Just as He was able to free Peter, He will free you from every bondage and stronghold of the adversary. Just as the devil failed

Prayer Focus

- ◆ Break off every chain and fetter that has held you bound to the same spot.

- ◆ Just as Peter's breakthrough came on the night before his trial, ask the Lord to give you a "right on time" breakthrough.

- ◆ Command gates of cities, businesses and organizations to begin to open for you.

concerning Peter, He will fail concerning you and your family. You will arise from the miry clay that is trying to make you sink. You will arise from everything that is trying to suck your life and your joy out of you. You will no longer be beaten, battered or trodden underfoot. You will no longer be down. You are empowered by the Holy Ghost to bulldoze your way out of the camp of the adversary. Nothing or no one will be able to limit or hold you down. Every wall or prison of limitation is broken down by the power of the Holy Ghost today in Jesus' name.

When you hear about mishaps, they will not be your portion in Jesus' name because your case is different. The Lord who preserved Peter and caused him to escape from the midst of over sixteen soldiers will make a way of escape for you. He who was faithful to loose every chain and fetter that bound Peter will loose every chain that has held you bound in Jesus' name. When Peter appeared to the Christians who were praying for him, they were surprised to see him. Your testimony will surprise many that know and don't know you. In Verse 18, the Bible says that there was commotion among the soldiers. The Lord will begin to trouble your troublers. He will give you victory on every side. The enemy will not have the last word over your life and destiny. He will not have the last word over your children. He will not have the last word over your health. Every plan he is concocting or has concocted has been foiled by the power of the Holy Ghost. Peter had an assignment; therefore the devil could not abort his destiny. You have an assignment and you are on an assignment. You will

Herod thought that he would succeed, taking and killing Peter just as he succeeded taking and killing James; but the Lord said it was not Peter's time. The Lord that said it was not Peter's time is saying to you too that it is not your time yet. It is not your time to die. You will not be defeated. You will not be put to shame.

fulfill God's plan and purpose for your life. You will not go before your time. Doors of cities and nations will open for you effortlessly in Jesus' name. Your days of struggling are over. The power of the Holy Spirit will loose you from all links to every generational curse that has affected your life in Jesus' name. You are breaking free of every stronghold of the enemy. The Lord will anoint you with the "breaker's" anointing. I hear the Lord saying, "Long standing problems will go away. Problems that have defied solutions will easily disappear. Your many years of struggling will be over. Your debts will be wiped away. Many will wonder what they have done to merit this. It is going to be a season of grace." He is saying, "There is coming a season of the release of God's power that will take away sicknesses. There will be a season of release that will cause little to become plenteous and a season of unending joy and great grace. Many that have been toiling endlessly will begin to see things become easy. It shall be a season of favor for many, but a season of judgment against wickedness." You are too hot to handle in Jesus' name!

Reference Scripture
"Behold, they shall surely gather together, but not by me: whosoever shall gather together against thee shall fall for thy sake" - Isaiah 54:15.

28

9

From Glory to Glory

Haggai 2:2-9

In the passage mentioned above, the Lord sent Haggai, the prophet, to speak to Zerubbabel, Joshua and to the residue of the people of Israel. He said those that were left saw the house "temple" in its former glory. He brought their attention to its present state. He asked them to compare its former state to its present condition. There was such a big difference!!! In their eyes, its present state looked like nothing compared to its former. God gave them a word of encouragement; a word that would change their lives forever. The word reassured them that God was still with them. Just as the Lord gave them a word of encouragement, He is giving you a word today. He says, "Be strong, I am with you. It doesn't matter how or what it looks like now; be strong for I am with you. I am not going to judge you by what you look like right now or where you are right now. You may have made some wrong turns that have brought you to the point you are at present. The enemy may have done some things, and he thinks it is over for you. I am still with you. It does not matter to Me what people think of you right now: I am not going to abandon you just because they have abandoned you. I am not going to put you aside or look down on you because of what people say or think about you. They did not create you. I did!!! Your destiny is not in their hands. It is in Mine!! You are my "temple" regardless of what state you are in. You are still Mine. I will be with you. I will remake you. I will re-mold you. I will form you after My will. I will live in you and make you My

> It does not matter to Me what people think of you right now. I am not going to abandon you just because they have abandoned you. I am not going to put you aside or abandon you because of what people say or think about you. They did not create you; I did!!! Your destiny is not in their hands; it is in Mine!! You are my temple regardless of what state you are in. You are still mine. I will be with you. I will remake you. I will re-mold you. I will form you after my will. I will live in you and still make you My glorious habitation.

Prayer Focus

- Ask the Lord to restore Hisglory back into the Church.
- Declare that the Church will begin to do what it has been called to do-win souls, bind up the broken hearted, heal the sick, seek the lost, deliverance to the oppressed, etc.
- Ask the power of the Holy Ghost to steer your life in the direction of your destiny.
- Ask the Lord to restore His glory back into your life.
- Declare the Church will become relevant again in God's end-time program.
- Ask the Holy Spiritto restore every covenant He has for you.

Spirit is with you. I will shake the heavens, the Earth, the seas and the dry land because of you. Did I not create these things? Did I not put them all under your charge? Do they not all have ears to hear you and obey you when you speak? I will shake them all for your glory. The silver is Mine and so is the gold. The Earth is Mine and all that dwell in it. I will shake them all because of you. I will fill your life with my glory. Everything that you need belongs to me. Your latter end will be more glorious

glorious habitation. I will do a new thing in you. I will beautify your life and I will revive you again"

"I will give you peace and make you a source of envy to many. They that come to you will find peace, solace and refuge. Trust Me. Obey Me and yield yourself completely to Me. You are the stone that was abandoned. You will now become a corner stone for many in your workplace, in your family and in your community. Be strong. Your latter end will definitely be greater than your former end."

"People that knew you in your former glory are comparing where you are now to what you were in the past. Don't worry; don't fret and don't be discouraged. Be strong; I am still with you. I am making a covenant with you, and I will not go back on my Word. My

Make the following declarations:

My latter end will be more glorious than my former in Jesus' name. I am not a "should have been." Where I am today will be the least I will ever be in my life. My destiny will not be aborted. I will finish my course. God will replace my ashes with His beauty. I will arise and shine for God's glory is upon me in the mighty name of Jesus. AMEN.

than your former. Where you are today is not your end and you will not end there. I will not leave you until I finish all I said I will do in you and through you. You are the apple of My eye. The desire of many will be yours because you will enjoy My favor. Be strong. Obey me. Love me. Fear Me. Believe Me; I am with you." saith the Lord.

Reference Scripture

"The glory of this latter house shall be greater than of the former, saith the LORD of hosts: and in this place will I give peace, saith the LORD of hosts" - Haggai 2:9. (KJV)

10

Out of the Heart!

Matthew 15:1-20

Some Scribes and Pharisees came to Jesus accusing Him that His disciples transgressed the tradition of the elders because they did not wash their hands before they ate. Jesus made them understand that they should be more concerned about people transgressing the commandments of God rather than the commandments of man. He goes on to explain to them that it is not what goes into a man's mouth that defiles him, but what comes out of it. Why? It is because what comes out of the mouth flows from his heart. Out of the heart flows all that defiles man such as adultery, fornication, backbiting, murder, false witness, and gossiping. He is saying that there are many that worship Him with their mouths, but their hearts are very far from Him. He is saying that our hearts matter to heaven more than our lips. God says that He is looking for true worshippers. He is saying enough is enough of those worshipping Him for what they can get from Him rather than worshipping Him for Who He is. Are you worshipping the gift or the Giver of the gift? Is the gift more important to you than the Giver of the gift? Will you still worship

Make the following declarations:

I command every door of opportunity to begin to open now in Jesus' name. I command every opportunity that I have lost in the past to begin to seek me out. I cast out of my life and family every spirit of abandonment and shame. My defeats are turning into triumphs. My life will become a testimony for many to envy. I receive joy where there has been bitterness and sorrow. God's hand is beginning to re-write my story from failure to success; from being a victim to being a victor. My life will please God. The Spirit of God will purge my heart in Jesus' name.

Him and will He still be your God if that husband, job, child, breakthrough, contract, money, or promotion He promised does not come?

Are you true worshipper? Are you one that needs to be 'hyped' by the sensationalism going on in the Church today for you to worship God? Are you a church hopper, a church "goer" a "bench warmer" or a worshipper? Do you go from pastor to pastor looking for miracles while ignoring the One that gives the miracles?

As a teacher or preacher of the word, do your messages edify the Word (Jesus) or are they enticing words of men? Are they God-centered or are they words that only 'hype' your congregation? Are the words kingdom-driven or religion-driven? Are they geared towards the traditions of men or towards the commandments of God? Are you a "men pleaser" or a "God pleaser" Are your words good seeds that are needed for the harvest, or are they words that deter or prevent many from the kingdom? Are working to fill your pews or to add souls to the kingdom? Sometimes your words as a preacher may offend men, but if they please God, you are okay.

God is saying, "I am a jealous God. I am looking for people who will worship Me in spirit and in truth. I do not want to share My glory with anyone or anything. I am looking for those who will worship Me in season and out of season; when it is convenient and when it is not. I am looking for those

Prayer Focus

◆ Ask the Lord to re-direct the church to Him, her "first love."

◆ Ask the Holy Spirit to begin to burn off everything that has been contending with God's love in your life.

◆ Frustrate, destroy and cancel every plan of the enemy against the end-time Church.

◆ The Bible in Matthew 24:12, the love of many will wax cold. Pray that your love for God and righteousness will wax stronger each day.

Prayer Focus

◆ Identify the weaknesses in your life and pray that the Lord will strengthen you so that you can overcome them.

◆ Pray against every set up by the enemy to distract you from your calling and assignment.

◆ Pray that the Lord will strengthen and uphold your pastor.

who will worship Me with their lips, their hearts and their actions. I am looking for those who will preach the truth in season and out of season. I am looking for those whose motives are pure and those whose words match their actions. I will do a new thing for those who will shift their focus to Me and away from man; those who will shift their focus away from things. I will do a new thing for those who will go back to their first love, Me." God is asking, "What or who is your first love? Is it Me or is it what I can give? For I am looking at the heart and I will reward my people according to the condition of it. I will separate the wheat from the tare."

Reference Scripture

"But the hour cometh, and now is, when the true worshippers shall worship the Father in spirit and in truth: for the Father seeketh such to worship him" – John 4:23.(KJV)

1

Speak the blessings below into your life. Receive each blessing and declare them over and over.

- My struggles are over. Many years of labor, unfruitfulness and barrenness will cease in my life.

- The Lord will crown my efforts with great success.

- I shall recover all the enemy has stolen from me.

- The Lord will satisfy me early with His goodness, blessings, prosperity, sound health and abundant peace.

- He will load me daily with His benefits.

- The gates of glory, honor and divine lifting will be opened unto me.

- I will enjoy rest on every side.

- I will not labor in vain; I will not labor for trouble.

- God's wind will part every Red Sea of my life.

- Every door that has been shut against me will begin to open effortlessly.

- I will enter into my inheritance. I will walk into my breakthrough.

- Every day of my life will be better than the day before.

◈ The Lord will give me supernatural strength and boldness to go after my adversary.

◈ I will soar to great heights like the Eagle; nothing will be too hard for me.

◈ I will see like God wants me to see; I will experience all God wants me to experience.

◈ I will enjoy divine wisdom; the Lord will make me a solution center to many.

◈ I will move to the next level spiritually, financially, academically, materially and in all areas of my life.

◈ I will become a positive point of reference for everyone that knows me.

◈ My head will be lifted and the Lord will banish every source of sorrow. The mighty hand of the Lord will wipe away tears of sorrow and cause my season of rejoicing to appear.

◈ God's mighty hand will roll away every stone of reproach and shame.

◈ I command great grace and peace upon my family and I in Jesus' name.

◈ My destiny is inevitable.

◈ The Earth will yield her increase to me.

◈ I am strategically lined up with the ladder from the Earth that touches the 3rd heaven. Angels will ascend and descend according to the words that I speak.

◈ I will ride daily on the wings of the Eagle into my days of victory and breakthrough.

◈ God's glory will erupt in my life and beautify my life.

◈ It shall be well with me body, soul and spirit. God's peace be unto me in Jesus' name. AMEN.

11

Honey in Your Carcass!

Judges 14:5-9

Samson was on his way to Timnath when a young lion roared at him. He did not run; he tore the lion into pieces with his bare hands. When he walked by the place some days later, he discovered the carcass of the lion. In it were two things- a swarm of bees that could sting him and honey that was food for him. Samson encountered a situation that should have scared him. Instead of running, he went for the honey.

> How are you handling the situations confronting you during these economic times? Are you running from them.....or are you taking the good out of the bad; looking for the opportunities in a bad situation? Just as Samson was able to get the honey out of the carcass of the lion in spite of the bees in the carcass, God is expecting us to begin to see our adversities as opportunities in disguise.
>
> **Prayer Focus**
> - Ask the Lord to open your spiritual eyes to see all He wants you to see.

How are you handling the situations confronting you during these economic times? Are you running from them? Are you looking for excuses not to confront them, or are you taking the good out of the bad? Are you looking for the opportunities in a bad situation? Just as Samson was able to get the honey out of the carcass of the lion in spite of the bees, God is expecting you to begin to see your adversities as opportunities in disguise. He is expecting you to transform your experiences into new lessons to learn. These lessons will lead you to the next level in ministry, in business, in your relationships, in your home, in your career and in every area of your life. If you run, you cannot learn, you cannot grow and the changes you want to see will not happen. If you run, you will keep on running!!!

We are being faced daily with challenges in life, in ministry and in our homes. We face financial challenges, marital challenges, and many others. God wants us to be able to transform these challenges into breakthroughs. Can you, like Samson, go after the honey in your carcass?

Prayer Focus

♦ Ask the power of the Holy Spirit to begin to fling open new doors of opportunities in business, relationship, ministry, etc. for you.

♦ Declare you will walk into your inheritance. You will not miss your day of visitation.

♦ Every negative ordinance against your destiny is aborted in Jesus' name.

Can you see God in action in your life and home even in spite of all that is happening around you? Can you look at your challenges and say you have learned the lessons God wants you to learn from them or are you complaining and griping about what has been or what should have been? Most importantly, He wants you to apply every lesson you learn. It is when we apply the lessons that we have wisdom.

In the midst of the economic crisis, people are losing their homes, their jobs, families and all, but God is beginning to infuse His wisdom into those who are ready for the honey. He is giving wisdom to those who are learning their lessons from all that is happening around them and putting the lessons into action. He is looking for those who will look for opportunities for greatness in their adversity. Those who will look at problems and see them as opportunities. He is looking for those who will not sit and complain about who did what, what should have happened and what did not happen, He is looking for people who will not play the "blame game", have the "victim mentality" and give up on their hopes and dreams. Steve Maraboli said, "The problem that we have with victim mentality is that we forget to see the blessings of the day. Because of this, our spirit is poisoned instead of nourished."

Prayer Focus

♦ Not all that looks bad is bad; ask the Lord for the Spirit of discernment.

♦ Ask the Lord to anoint you afresh with His Spirit of wisdom, knowledge and understanding.

♦ Ask for the anointing to transform your challenges into breakthroughs.

Are you one of those that God can trust with His life transforming lessons? Can you be faithful to put into action all He is showing you and telling you to do? May He open your ears to hear and your eyes to see. May your adversity not crush you, but be stepping stones to your greatness. May every opportunity be life transforming to you. You will not miss it. You will not be a "should have been" in Jesus 'name. You will not miss any divine lessons God wants you to learn. You will do great and mighty things in your home, in your church, in your workplace and in your business. You will do great and mighty things in your generation and in the kingdom of God. Although you may have been a victim; like Samson, you will be able to overcome all odds to get your honey and become a victor. Where others are failing you will succeed in Jesus' name.

Reference Scripture

Behold, I have set before thee an open door, and no man can shut it: for thou hast a little strength, and hast kept my word, and hast not denied my name. – Revelation 3:8

12

You Shall See and Surely Possess!

Deuteronomy 34:1-5

It is a sad thing to see a good thing and not to be a partaker of it. The above passage talks about Moses' last days. He went to the top of a mountain, and God began to show him the land He promised his fathers, Abraham, Isaac and Jacob and their seed. God said even though He showed Moses the land, Moses would not be able to cross over and enter into it. What a disappointment! It is a grave thing in the case of Moses to suffer the way he did for 40 years to lead a people to the Promised Land and not to enter into it.

> It is a grave thing in the case of Moses to suffer the way he did for 40 years to lead a people to the Promised Land and not to enter into it.
>
> It is also a much sadder case, for you to work in the vineyard for so many years, laboring in the choir, usher board, preaching and doing all you have to do and not making it to heaven at last!!!

The same thing happened in II Kings 7:1-20 when Elisha pronounced that in 24 hours there was going to be an economic transformation in Samaria. The man upon whom the king leaned did not believe it. Most times when you fail an examination, it is either because you do not know anything or because you do not know enough! It was either this man did not know the God of Elisha or he did not know enough about the bigness of the God of Elisha. He was ignorant. He told Elisha that it was impossible. Elisha's response was, "Thou shall see it with your eyes, but shall not eat of it." It is also sad in the case of this man who saw so much food after such a long period of deprivation and starvation, but still was not able to eat any of it. This will not be your portion in Jesus' name. It is sad living in the midst of plenty and not being a partaker of it. It is also a much sadder case for you to work in the vineyard for so many years, laboring in the choir, on the usher board, preaching and doing all you have to do, and not making it to heaven at last!!! It is also very sad to hear all that the Lord wants to do in your life and not enjoy or be a partaker of it. It is sad to fail on the verge of success. It is sad to hear about God's promises and not possessing them.

You have labored so much in your life, you must reap. You have worked hard; it will not be in vain. You have labored much over your children; they will not die at the prime of their lives. They will not be negative points of reference to other kids. You will live to see their good. As the enemy is looking for ways for the children of God to miss it, you will not miss it in Jesus' name. You will believe and trust Him for all He has said to you. You will hear, see and enjoy the good of the land. The Lord will cause you to enjoy every promise He has for you. You will not experience poverty in the midst of plenty. You will not experience sickness while others are receiving their healing. He will prepare you for all that He has prepared for you. Life, pressures, challenges and the enemy will not take you before your time. Moses' character flaw, anger, made him miss his promised land. The man upon whose shoulder the king leaned in II Kings 7 did not make it because of unbelief and ignorance.

You will not prevent yourself from getting to your promised land in Jesus' name. I curse to the roots anything in your life that can deter your promotion or progress and anything that can destroy your joy and peace in Jesus' name. I root out everything in your life that will make you to see and not to possess in Jesus' name. I plead the blood of Jesus upon you. You will be singled out as one of those who will hear, believe, see, enter in and possess in Jesus' name. You will see all that God wants you to see. You will possess all that He wants you to possess. You will possess all heaven has

Prayer Focus

♦ Ask the Holy Spirit to begin to water every seed you have sown that has refused to germinate.

♦ Declare that the Lord will renew your strength.

♦ Command God's rain to cause your seeds to bear fruit that will abide.

♦ Ask the Holy Spirit to remove every character flaw that will abort your destiny.

♦ Frustrate every plan of the enemy to cause you to labor in the vineyard and not reap the fruit.

Prayer Focus

♦ Ask the Lord to begin to reward you for all your years of labor in His vineyard, in your home, work place, school, or community.

♦ Pray that you will not suffer lack in the midst of plenty.

Prayer Focus

- Destroy every plan of the enemy to cause you to experience fruitless labor, defeat, shame and failure.

- Ask the Holy Spirit to purge you of any character flaw that will prevent you from entering into your land of promise.

- Prophesy that your tomorrow will be better than your today in the mighty and precious name of Jesus.

released to you on this side of eternity. You will possess the land of your anointing. Your land is your health, job, home, marriage, children, ministry, business, and your school......Your land will yield fruit to you spiritually, financially, economically, materially, academically, professionally, and in all areas. It will yield her increase to you. You will not labor in that office for someone else to reap the fruits of your labor. You will not labor in that marriage for someone else to reap the fruit of your labor. You will not labor in that ministry or church for someone else to reap the fruit of your labor. You will not labor here on Earth and miss your heavenly crown in Jesus' name. You will possess the land of your adversary. The heavens will open her windows unto you and cause you to enjoy favor you have not enjoyed before. Whatever is yours, death will not take it away; sickness will not take it away; the challenges you are facing today will not take it away; disobedience will not take it away; neither will sin take it away. You will possess your possession. You will fulfill your

Reference Scripture
"They shall not build, and another inhabit; they shall not plant, and another eat: for as the days of a tree are the days of my people, and mine elect shall long enjoy the work of their hands"-Isaiah 65:22.

13

Without Fail, You Shall Recover All

I Samuel 30:1-18

Several things may be happening in your life that look as if it is no use trying anymore. You are saying to yourself, "It is over; I will begin again some other time." I am saying to you. "It is not the time to give up on God because He has not given up on you." In the above passage, David was away from Ziklag with his men and the Amalekites came to invade the city. They took all their wives and children and everything they owned. On the third day, David and his men came back and discovered what had happened. They were all very distressed. His men were so affected by it, they were going to stone him to death. David knew that unless something drastic and miraculous happened, he was going to lose his position as captain over his men. He was going to lose his reputation. He was going to be disgraced and put to shame. This would mean that he had failed in the assignment God had given him as captain over his men. The Bible records in I Samuel 22:2 that these 400 men that followed David had issues: They were in distress, in debt and discontented. They followed him because they looked up to him and believed in him. He was in a predicament. What should he do? He was also discouraged, grieved and distressed, but because of his men's sake, he had to get up from his pity party. He had to take a drastic measure. He encouraged himself in the Lord and called on God. David asked God two questions, "Do I pursue? Will I overtake?" God gave him three

> David knew that unless something drastic and miraculous happened, he was going to lose his position as captain over his men. He was going to lose his reputation. He was going to be disgraced and put to shame. This would mean that he had failed in the assignment that God had given him as captain over his men......He was in a predicament. What should he do?........He called on God. ....David pursued, he overtook and recovered all that was taken from him.....He did not only take all that was his, he was able to take his enemy's stuff too!

answers: "Pursue, You will surely overtake and without fail recover all." What an answer!!! What an assurance!!! David pursued, he overtook and recovered all that was taken from him. There was nothing missing, nothing broken and nothing lacking. He recovered all that belonged to him and his men and he was able to take the enemy's stuff too!

Prayer Focus

♦ Ask the power of the Holy Ghost to begin to blow your way everything you have lost spiritually, physically, materially, financially and emotionally in Jesus' name.

♦ Ask the Lord to turn your set back into a set up for your breakthrough.

♦ Declare that the anointing will reverse any negative handwriting over your life and destiny.

♦ Ask Him to make this a season of recovery for you.

♦ Declare that the enemy will not have the last word over your life and family.

♦ Declare that many that have looked down at you will begin to look up to you.

♦ Declare all that you have lost will come back with interest.

♦ Declare that heaven will back you up and give you the wealth of the wicked.

Have you found yourself in a predicament and it looks like if God does not do something quickly, you will fall flat on your face, disgraced and put to shame? Are people saying that if you have really been called, or if you are really a Christian, you should not be experiencing all the chaos, confusion and disappointments you are facing in your life? Are they saying, "If he cannot help himself, how can he help us?" The Bible says that it was on the third day that David discovered that their wives and children had been abducted. Spiritually, the Number 3 represents the Trinity (Father, Son and Holy Ghost). The Number 3 represents celebration, rejoicing and jubilation. Jesus rose on the 3rd day. His rising and resurrection represents celebration for all Christians today. When David and his men were supposed to be rejoicing, they received bad news of their loss. But the Lord reversed it for them. The Lord that did it for David will reverse every plan of the enemy to make you weep or sorrow in Jesus' name. When you are supposed to rejoice, the enemy wants you to mourn. But the Lord is saying, "Encourage yourself in Me and you will weep no more. Your bosses, co-workers, friends, and people who have seen you distressed will begin to see My glory in your life again. People who have seen you down will begin to see you rise again." God says that you will recover your peace, your joy, your reputation, your honor and glory, your health, your home, your child, your spouse, your job and your relationships that the enemy has stolen. You will recover all that he has stolen and you will take his stuff too!!! The wealth of the wicked is laid up for you (Proverbs 13:22). Just as David was able to come out of his pity party, God is calling you out of yours. He is saying, "That situation will not end up in disgrace." He is calling you out of the miry clay. He is setting your feet upon a rock. He is establishing your goings and putting a new song of victory in your mouth! (Psalm 40:2). People who have despised you because of a little set back will celebrate you again. People who think you have nothing to say will listen to you, and they will follow you. God is making you a mystery no one can solve. You are that solution center your family, co-workers, church, ministry, subdivision and the world is waiting for.

Has your heart been broken? The Lord will heal it. Has your reputation and integrity been tarnished? You will recover them. Has your peace been stolen? You will recover it. Has the devil taken your home, finances and health? You will recover them. Has the devil slapped you in the face? He will pay for it double!!! The devil cannot and will not take you out. You will not be put to shame. You will not be disgraced. It is your season of recovery. It is your season of restoration. It is your season to take back all the enemy has taken from you due to your carelessness, ignorance and error. Just ask for God's mercy. It shall be well. He is restoring the years the enemy has stolen from you. He is restoring those opportunities you have missed. He is restoring your mind. Your stuff is coming back with interest in Jesus' name. **AMEN**.

Reference Scripture
"And I will restore to you the years that the locust hath eaten, the cankerworm, and the caterpillar, and the palmerworm, my great army which I sent among you" - Joel 2:25.

14

Solutions Not Resolutions

"There has never been the slightest doubt in my mind that the God who started this great work in you would keep at it and bring it to a flourishing finish on the very day Christ Jesus appears" Philippians 1:6. (The Message Translation)

Every New Year, people make resolutions about different areas of their lives. It is their desire to have a closer walk with God, lose some weight, work on relationship issues, and even prioritize certain things in their lives. However, midway they become tired, discouraged, frustrated, lose focus and all these resolutions are thrown unintentionally out of the window. Perhaps you did not fulfill all your goals in the past years; every day is a new beginning. Every day is a new day of the manifestation of His Word in your life. In Genesis 1:2, God's Spirit moved upon the Earth. God saw darkness, but He wanted to see light; so He spoke what He wanted to see into existence. He divided light from darkness (action). He saw a need to separate the waters which were above from the waters which were beneath. So He spoke and then He acted on His Word. What do you want to see in the coming days? Begin to speak into your life, destiny, home, job, career, business, ministry, or children what you want to see.

Prayer Focus

- Frustrate the spirit of "abandoned projects," chaos and confusion in your life.
- Ask for the Spirit of an accomplisher to rest on you.
- Ask the Holy Spirit to lead and direct you andcause you to see allyou have spoken into existence.
- Pray that the Lord will help you to be true to Him and to yourself.

Whatever solutions you resolve to see must be permanent, and they will be in Jesus name. Make decisions and stick to them! What would the world be like if God had aborted the whole process in the middle of creation? Chaotic! What He started, He completed. That is why we can see the Earth manifest His glory. You too are His creation. You will manifest His glory. Speak to that situation and then take your step of faith (action). Over time you will see the manifestations. Don't give up, give out or give in. If there are issues that you need to address, address them and stick to your decisions. If there are relationships that you need to cut off, do it and stick to it. Each New Year, you are embarking on a glorious journey. If you start well and you determine not to quit mid-way, you will definitely finish well. Ask God to help you stick to the decisions you make. Ask Him to open your eyes to things you have to do and things you need to change. Pray for strength and He will give it to you. Quitters never win. Winners never quit. Don't just talk about the change, be about it. The Word brought the world into existence. The Word will uphold you; especially when you feel like you cannot make it. I see you walking victoriously. May each new day of your life be better than the day before it. May you enjoy God's favor and His presence daily. May your life be a blessing to your generation and to generations after you. You are on your way to the other side and you will get there in Jesus name. **AMEN**.

Prayer Focus

♦ Pray that heaven will help you to do all that you say you will do.

♦ Pray you will not be weary. Receive divine strength in the name of Jesus.

♦ Declare strength to replace weakness.

♦ Pray that everything God created will work in your favor in Jesus' name.

Reference Scripture

"Being confident of this very thing, that he which hath begun a good work in you will perform it until the day of Jesus Christ"- Philippians 1:6.

47

Inspirational Quotes

2

◆ "I will persist until I succeed. Always will I take another step. If that is of no avail, I will take another, and yet another. In truth, one step at a time is not too difficult. I know that small attempts, repeated, will complete any undertaking." –Og Mandino

◆ "What lies behind us and what lies before us are small matters compared to what lies within us."- Ralph Waldo Emerson

◆ "If you see darkness all around you, God has given you the opportunity to shine your own special light. You are the light the world wants to see." - Anonymous

◆ "Don't sacrifice to God what He has not asked for. To obey is better than to sacrifice." - Anonymous

◆ "Healthy compromise is not giving up what you believe in, who you are, or accepting the second best because you are impatient or afraid of criticism." - Anonymous

◆ "If you change the way you look at things, the things you look at will change." - Anonymous

◆ "The road to greatness is lined up with many tempting parking spaces." – Anonymous

◆ "A wise man in a storm prays to God not for safety from danger, but for deliverance from fear." – Anonymous

◆ "The cave you fear to enter holds the treasure you seek." - Anonymous

◆ "Never close the book of your life when God has not finished writing." - Anonymous

- "There is nothing as useless as doing efficiently that which should not have been done at all." – Anonymous

- Don't judge a person by what others say. The person may be true to you, but not to others because the sun that melts the ice hardens the clay." - Anonymous

15

Is Jesus in It?

John 21:1-6

After Jesus' death, Peter called some disciples to go fishing with him. They toiled all night and caught nothing. Peter was an experienced fisherman. It did not make sense that after all the many hours of toiling he still did not catch anything. I can imagine how he must have felt; definitely frustrated and depressed. Then in the morning, Jesus shows up and asks them, "Do you have meat?" In essence, He was saying, "Do you have anything to show for your hours of labor and toiling?" Their answer was, "No." They were saying, "No, we have toiled in vain. We have been unfruitful. Our vessel is empty. We have worked but have nothing to show for it." The Jesus tells them exactly where to cast their net; on the right side of the ship. As soon as they obeyed, their labor of many hours was rewarded. What a blessing!!! What joy they must have felt. They did not only catch some fish, the Bible records they caught a multitude of fishes. Are you like Peter and the disciples, frustrated and tired after laboring and toiling so much in that business, in that marriage, in that church, and ministry with nothing to show for it? Just like the disciples, it is not that you do not know what to do or how to go about it; things are just not working out. It seems that the more you labor, the less you achieve. Sometimes when we become so good at a thing we begin to think we are successful because of what we know and what we can do. God sometimes will have to slow us down, humble us and show us we need Him. He wants to have a hand in and the last word over your life and in all that you do. He wants to take the glory in your life. Are you giving Him the glory He deserves? When you involve Him, He shows up. When

> They toiled all night and caught nothing. Then in the morning, Jesus shows up and asks him, "Do you have meat?" In essence, He was saying, "Do you have anything to show for your hours of labor and toiling? And Peter's answer was, "No".......Are you like Peter frustrated and tired after laboring and toiling so much in that business, in that marriage, in that church, or ministry with nothing to show for it?

Prayer Focus

♦ Release yourself into the hands of the Lord and tell Him you need Him more than you have ever needed Him.

♦ Ask Him to cause years of endless labor to cease.

♦ Destroy by the power of the Holy Ghost every spirit that has frustrated your life and efforts.

♦ Ask the Lord to enthrone Himself in your life and in everything that concerns you.

♦ Ask the Lord to make this season a season of joy and celebration for you.

♦ Ask the Lord to speedily manifest all that He has said concerning you.

♦ Pray that the wrap you in His favor.

♦ Begin to reject lack, frustration, fruitless labor, rejection, shame and reproach.

♦ Pray that as from today, all you lay your hands on will prosper in the mighty name of Jesus.

he shows up, fruitless labor and many years of toiling ceases and all you do begins to yield fruit. You, the recipient of the blessing will not be able to understand it. How much of your life do you involve Jesus? Who is in control; you or Him? On one occasion, Peter experienced a miracle like this. In Luke 5:1-11, he borrowed Jesus his boat to use to preach to the people. After Jesus was done, He said to Simon, *"Launch into the deep and let down your net for a drought."* Peter answered Jesus. *"Master, we have toiled all night and have taken nothing, nevertheless, at thy word......"* After they obeyed Jesus, they caught a multitude of fish. The fishes were so many, their net broke! After this miracle, Peter, James and John forsook all became disciples.

It was because Jesus was in their boat that they became fruitful fisher men. Then they invited Him into the "boat" of their lives and became disciples. Do you know that we can do the right thing, and still keep God out? It can be a good thing but it may not be a "God thing". Are you asking God to bless your decisions or are you asking Him to lead you on your journey? God wants to be invited to be the Sole Pilot, the Author and Finisher, the Beginning and the End and the Final Authority over the affairs of your life. Are you ready to surrender? Is He in your home? Is He in your ministry? Is He the One running your church or are you using all the knowledge you have learned to run it? Yes, you can preach very well: Is the message from Him? Yes, you can dance well: Is your performance in that dance group giving Him the glory? Are you dancing for Him? Are you a performer or a worshipper? Are you in that choir singing for Him or are you just doing it for yourself? Is He the One running your business? Is He the Owner of that business or is it you? Most importantly, is He the One running your life? If Jesus is in it, I see you working this season and gaining much. I see your efforts that have failed in the past yielding fruit; if you give Him complete authority and liberty. I see Him healing your marriage, prospering your business and growing your church or ministry. When Peter caught all that fish, it was his season of joy. I see you walking into your season of joy. Peter went from his season of lack into his season of abundance and fruitfulness. May you never labor in vain again and may the anointing for fruitfulness rest upon you. May you experience a divine encounter with the King of glory. You will not labor for loss. You will not labor for somebody else to reap. You will enjoy every fruit of your labor in Jesus' name. The journey that will take others ten years to travel will take you only one year. God will prosper your life. You will not only yield physical fruits, you will yield spiritual fruits. Many will come to know Jesus through you. Your life will become a testimony. Jesus will show up every time you need Him. Those things that did not work for you in the past will begin to work for you. When Jesus came into the picture, Peter's story changed. Your story will change. The Lord will re-write your destiny. The Lord will soften every hard ground and make it the land of your anointing and the land of your prosperity in Jesus' name. **AMEN**

Reference Scripture
"Beloved, I pray that you may prosper in all things and be in health, just as your soul prospers."-III John 2

16

Watch that Clock!

Matthew 25:6-13

The passage mentioned above talks about the story of five virgins that missed the opportunity to see the bridegroom they had supposedly been awaiting. Verse 6 says that at midnight, a cry came to alert them that the bridegroom was on his way. Unfortunately, they did not have any oil left in their lamps so they went looking for oil. By the time they came back, the bridegroom had come and gone and the door had been shut against them. They had lost a great opportunity! It was a big disappointment and there was nothing they could do about it. Sounds familiar?

God has been speaking constantly about opportunities, chances and timing. He is saying it again and again because He wants us to yield. My prayer is that the Lord will cause His Word to bear fruit in our lives. If the virgins had put oil in their lamps when they had the chance, they would not have missed the opportunity to enter, see, dine with the Bridegroom and enjoy all the benefits of the marriage feast!

> Have you noticed that you have been missing opportunities to do great things in the kingdom, in your work place, or in your home? ....There is a time in heaven and on earth for everything (Ecclesiastes 3:1). Every time the second or hour hand of the clock moves, it is time that has passed and can never be taken back. It represents opportunities lost that may never be regained. It is time that has refused to wait for you... God will not change His plan; He will only change the vessel. You will not be replaced in Jesus' name.

Have you noticed that you have been missing opportunities to do great things in the kingdom, in your workplace, in business and in your home? Ecclesiastes 3:1 says, *"To everything there is a season, and a time to every purpose under the heaven."* "There is a time in heaven and on Earth for everything. Every time the second or hour hand of the clock moves, it means time that has gone by and can never be taken back. It represents opportunities lost that may never be regained. It is time that has refused to wait for you. It means you must do what you have to do now and at the right time, or else someone else might be chosen to do it.

Have you done those things God has told you to do? If not, what are you waiting for? Have you made peace with that person? What is that unholy relationship you are desperately holding on to that He is telling you to break? What is He saying that you have ignored? Are you working on God's time or on your time? If you are working on your time, you will fail and fall flat on your face. It will not be your portion in Jesus' name.

God will not change His plan. He will only change the vessel. You will not be replaced in Jesus' name. God is saying, "Pay attention to the clock!!" He is saying, "Pay attention to the little details." It is through the little things that He has been speaking. It is through those little details that He is and He will be speaking to you. In II Kings 5, the little slave girl in Naaman's house was the one God used for Naaman's healing and deliverance. Are you listening?

God is saying, "Pay attention to the clock!!" He is saying, "Pay attention to the little details." It is through the little things thatHe has beenspeaking; it is through those little details that He is and He will be speaking to you.

God is saying, "If you are not born again, don't miss the opportunity to give your heart to Him. Don't miss the opportunity to minister salvation to that unsaved neighbor, co-worker or friend; tomorrow may be too late. Do not miss the opportunity to do a good deed. Do not miss out on the opportunity to make the difference in your workplace, home, or wherever you are. Get excited about God's word. Get excited about the Kingdom. Get excited

Prayer Focus

♦ Pray that your clock will not stop abruptly.

♦ Pray that your oil will not run out.

♦ Pray that your doors of opportunity will not be shut against you.

♦ Pray that heaven will release all you need to make it in life and ministry.

♦ Pray that your oil and anointing will not run dry, be compromised or contaminated.

♦ Pray for grace to serve the Lord all the way to the end in Jesus' name.

about your purpose and destiny! Get excited about your assignment! Get excited about where you will spend eternity (heaven), the final home for all Christians!!!"

Do not miss out on the opportunity to make your mark. Watch that clock; it is constantly ticking and its hands are moving!!! You never know when it will stop. It will not stop and meet you unprepared in Jesus' name. May God's anointing rest upon you and may the heavens open over your life. I decree grace to do exploit in and for the kingdom. I frustrate every spirit of discouragement and weariness. I frustrate every spirit of Luke warmness and doubt. I frustrate every spirit of procrastination in Jesus' name. I come against spiritual blindness in Jesus' name. You will not become irrelevant. You will not miss it in Jesus' name. May the Lord exalt your horn like the horn of a unicorn and anoint you with fresh oil. Your time will not run out before you accomplish your purpose. You are anointed for impact. Great grace is upon you. You will be so blessed that the blessed will call you blessed in Jesus' name.

Reference Scripture

"So teach us to number our days, that we may apply our hearts unto wisdom" – Psalm 90 12.

17

Time Out!

I Kings 19:1-16

In I Kings 18, Elijah had just won a battle of the "gods" on Mt. Carmel. He had killed 450 Prophets of Baal and everything was going on well for him. He must have felt good about himself and his accomplishment. God was with him. Suddenly, everything came crashing down. He received a threat from Jezebel that caused his head to spin and he took to his heels. Jezebel threatened to kill him within 24 hours because he killed the prophets of Baal and made a show of their gods. Out of fear, Elijah took to his heels. He runs a day's journey. Tired, frustrated, dejected, discouraged and ready to give up, he stops to rest at a Juniper tree. There, he begs God for death. Elijah had reached the end of the road and thought it was over for him. Remember, Jezebel's threat was to kill Elijah within 24 hours. By the time Elijah reached the

Prayer Focus

♦ Declare you will see all that the enemy says you will not see.

♦ Declare you will experience all that the enemy says that you will not experience.

♦ Declare the enemy's time is over in your life, home and ministry.

♦ Declare your life will negate every plan and purpose of the enemy.

Juniper tree, her time was up! It was over 24 hours!! Elijah was not supposed to see the Juniper tree, but he did! Sounds familiar? Where you are today is the last place the enemy wants you to be. When you look back, what you have done or where you have been in your life is not what the enemy planned for you. You were not meant to be conceived. You were

Prayer Focus

♦ Ask the Lord to feed you daily spiritually and lift you up from where you are.

♦ Cancel every appointment with of death over your life and family today in Jesus' name.

not meant to see your 1st, 10th, 20th or even your last birthday, but you did. You were not meant to graduate, but you did. You were not meant to survive that last heart attack or stroke, but you did. You were not meant to survive the surgery, but you did. You were not meant to have children or to see any of your children, but you did. You were not meant to survive cancer, but you did. You were not meant to give your life to Jesus, but you did. You were not meant to see this day, but you have. You are not meant to be where you are today, but you are. You were not meant to...........but guess what? You did, you have and you still are!!! Just as Jezebel's time was over in Elijah's life, the enemy's time is over in yours. The time of sicknesses and diseases is over in your life. The time of frustration is over in your life. The time of hopelessness is over in your life. The time of oppression and depression is over. The time of poverty is over in your life. The plan of the enemy will not prosper over you and your family in the mighty name of Jesus.

> Jezebel's threat was to kill Elijah in 24 hours. By the time Elijah reached the Juniper tree, her time was over!!! Elijah was not supposed to see the Juniper tree, but he did..... You were not meant to see your 1st, 10th, 20th or even your last birthday, but you did. You were not meant to....., but guess what? You did!

Prayer Focus

♦ Just as the enemy's time ran out in Elijah's life, pray that his time will run out in your life and family.

♦ Just as God opened Elijah's eyes to the work He wanted Him to do and a reason to live, you will receive a new anointing for the next level of your assignment.

♦ Pray that the Holy Host will refresh you for your next level in Jesus' name.

♦ Declare you will not be weary. You will ride upon the wings of the Eagle.

When Elijah was at his lowest, the Lord sent an angel to him to feed him. You will enjoy divine visitation. The Lord will feed you spiritually. He will feed you with His Word. He will feed you with wisdom, knowledge and understanding. He will give you all you need when you need it. We do not always get all we want, but God gives us all we need. Elijah wanted death, but God knew he needed to live to accomplish His plan and purpose, not only for his life but for others (I Kings 19:15-16). What are those things that God has in His plan for you that the enemy is fighting against? You will live to enjoy every plan and purpose God has for your life. You will enjoy God's rest and peace. The Ever

Prayer Focus

♦ Pray that God will do exceedingly abundantly above all that you ask or think in Jesus name.

♦ Pray that you will not fail, fall or falter.

♦ Pray the God will disappoint every antic, orchestration and machination of the enemy against you.

♦ Pray the Lord will put upon you the anointing of a champion.

Present Help will be your companion. You will not faint or fall. You will not be defeated. The rod of the wicked will not rest upon your lot (Psalm 125:3). You will live to see everything the enemy says you will not see. You will enjoy all that he says you will not enjoy. Your life will be contrary to all that he has planned in Jesus' name. When he says there is a casting down, you will experience a lifting up. When he speaks death, you shall live. When he speaks sorrow, there will be joy for you and your family. When He speaks drought, there will be abundance. God will give you victory over all of his plans in Jesus' name. **AMEN**.

Reference Scripture
"I shall not die, but live, and declare the works of the LORD" Psalm 118:17.

18

When God Does not Make Sense

There are many of us who have gone through our stuff in the past years and are still going through stuff. Most times it looks like a never ending cycle. Are you going through life thinking God has forgotten you? Be encouraged. Have you prayed and done everything you should do and nothing seems to be working? Be encouraged. Do you know that when God delays, He is not inactive?

God has promised that He will place you where He has prepared for you. Can you trust Him to do just that? Joseph...endured a long trial. But he was eventually placed in the palace when he was ready. Joseph was tested, but he continued to be faithful. He learned lessons on faithfulness, integrity, service, obedience and the fear of the Lord. He became someone with great wisdom; one many could depend on. God often has to burn the lessons we learn into the depth of our being. God refines us in our times of trial.

I heard the story of a man who lost his home, job and everything he had in 1991. He was distraught and he wondered why God would abandon him, He could not believe God would allow all those things to befall him in the same year. In 1995, four years after his demise, he got married, got a much better paying job and he bought a bigger and more beautiful house. He discovered that this new house was actually built in 1991 at the time he was going through his stuff. The house was unoccupied since then and God just reserved it especially for him. His new wife moved into the city where he lived the same year. God had prepared this dream home and a loving wife for him in 1991. All that he went through was to bring him to a point in 1995 when he was ready for all the Lord had prepared for him. In the years he was waiting, he gave his life to Christ and was maturing in the new relationship with Jesus his Lord and Savior.

Do you know that when He delays, He is preparing you for something big? Do you also know that when it looks like there is a delay, He is preparing you as an instrument and maturing your strength and faith in Him? God is never in a hurry, but He is always on time. He spends time preparing those He plans to use greatly.

In John 11 it did not make sense that Jesus did not rush immediately to Lazarus' house when He heard that Lazarus, His friend was sick. Verse 6 says that He waited two days where he was. Why did He have to wait two days? When He eventually reached his friends, Mary and Martha, Lazarus had been dead four days. It made no sense that He waited four days! Where was He when they desperately needed Him? His response to those who gave Him the news of His friend's sickness was, *"This sickness is not unto death, but for the glory of God that the Son of God might be glorified."* But Lazarus

Prayer Focus

- Declare that the pain and suffering you have suffered all your life will not be in vain.
- Pray that the lessons God wants you to learn will not elude you.
- Ask the Lord to renew your strength daily to wait on Him.
- Declare prosperity in the midst of famine.
- Pray for grace not to sabotage your destiny because of temporary pleasures.
- Ask the Holy Spirit, your Teacher to teach you daily in the name of Jesus.

died! I'm sure his sisters were thinking, what glory will this bring to You since our brother is dead? In their frustration, they told Jesus, *"If you had been here, our brother would not have died."* I believe both sisters were upset to the point that Mary stayed in the house and did not go to meet Jesus when she heard He had come. When God doesn't make sense and you don't feel like talking to Him, TALK TO HIM! In the end, Lazarus was raised up and God's name was glorified. It

Prayer Focus

- Ask the Lord to purify you so that He can see His image in you.
- Pray that every hurt and pain that you have gone through will begin to work out for your good.
- Ask God for grace to wait on Him, even in the midst of your storm.

may not make any sense, but just trust the process; trust God and He will be glorified in your life in Jesus' name.

> God is never in a hurry, but He is always on time... What you have gone through in the past is not in vain... Joseph was tested, but he continued to be faithful. He learned lessons on faithfulness, integrity, service, obedience and the fear of the Lord.

In the book of Genesis Joseph endured a long trial. It did not make sense for someone to do the right thing and still be thrown in the prison. When His time came, He was eventually placed in the palace. Joseph was tested, but he continued to be faithful. He passed his tests. He learned lessons on faithfulness, integrity, service, obedience and the fear of the Lord. He became someone with great wisdom; one many could depend on.

God often has to burn the lessons we learn into the depth of our being. God refines us in our times of trial and adversity. He prepares us so that we can shine for Him. He is a refiner and the purifier of silver. (Malachi 3:3). Like a true Silversmith, God stops the fire the moment He sees His image glowing in us.

Focus on the lessons you have learned and the ones you are learning. They will become very relevant as the Lord takes you on your journey to your destiny. Be encouraged, it will definitely get better!!!

In Genesis 26:12, Isaac prospered in the midst of famine. You will prosper in the midst of the current economic crisis and drought. You may be unable to see the final outcome of the beautiful plan that God has hidden in the shadow of His hand for you (Is 49:2), but it will surely come to pass. Today, it may be concealed; let your faith rest in the assurance that if He promised it, He will do it. He will not leave you or forsake you.

I am sure when Joseph got to the palace, he was able to look back and say, "All things have worked together for my good." It did not just work for his good, it worked for the good of his father, brothers and entire family! Many are the afflictions of the righteous, but the Lord delivered him from them all (Psalm 34:19). Be encouraged and assured of the good plans of the Ever Present, All Knowing and loving God and because of this assurance, you can calmly wait for a time when you can boldly say, "All things have worked together for my good!!!" There will be times that God will not make sense. Trust in Romans 8:28; it will surely work together for your good in Jesus' name. **AMEN.**

Scripture Reference

"And we know that all things work together for good to them that love God, to them who are the called according to his purpose"- Romans 8:28.

19

Herod Watch Out!!

When King Herod heard this he was disturbed, and all Jerusalem with him. When he had called together all the people's chief priests and teachers of the law, he asked them where the Christ was to be born. Matthew 2:3-4. (NKJV)

King Herod heard that a king was to be born. He was not happy because there could only be one king on the throne in Jerusalem, him. Someone who could take his place was to be born, and he desperately had to do something about it. He went on a rampage killing male babies in an attempt to kill baby Jesus. Herod heard a star had been born, and he wanted to destroy that star. He saw promise and destiny and sought to abort it. He wasn't going to wait until the child grew up. He was determined to end it now. Have you ever started a project and discovered at the beginning no matter how hard you tried, it would not take off? However, when you refuse to give up and continue to work at it, it eventually takes off and blossoms? Herod was going after this destiny at the beginning, and he knew if he succeeded that would be the end of it.

The enemy wants to prevent and stifle anything and everything God is doing or is in the process of doing in your life. John 10:10 says that he has come to steal, kill and destroy. Have you ever wondered why the enemy is going after you with so much fury? Are you looking at your life wondering why he is after you and not after the big fish? Guess what? Just as he saw little Jesus as a big fish, he sees you as one.

Herod heard a star had been born and he wanted to destroy that star. He saw promise and destiny and sought to abort it. He wasn't going to wait until the child grew up, he was going to do it now. Have you ever started a project and discovered at the beginning no matter how hard you tried, it would not take off? However, when you refuse to give up and continue to work at it, it eventually takes off and blossoms? Herod was going after this destiny at the beginning and he knew if he succeeded that would be the end of it.

Do not look down on yourself. Even if you don't know it, the devil knows you, and he knows what you are capable of becoming. He is determined not to allow you to get there. He does not care who or what he has to destroy in order to get to you. I declare in Jesus' name he will not prevail. I declare his plan over your life will be terminated. God will stop him in his tracks! The spies in Numbers 13 saw themselves as grasshoppers and the occupants of the land they were to possess as giants. May the Lord open your eyes to see how He sees you. You are big in His eyes and the devil will not be able to touch you or abort your destiny.

Although Joseph and Mary had to flee with Jesus, they returned to Jerusalem after a while because an angel told them that all that were after Jesus were dead. The enemy's plan over your life will not prosper. Whatever is meant to terminate your life will be terminated in Jesus' name. Whatever has terrorized you will be terrorized in Jesus' name. Your life, home, marriage, children, business, career, ministry and destiny are hid with Christ in God (Colossians 3:3). Is there a Herod in your life? He has to get to Jesus in order to get to you. He has to destroy Jesus to get to you. The King that sits on the throne of your life is immovable and cannot be dethroned. God's hand will rest upon you. He will shield you under His wings. He will destroy every Herod that is after your destiny. I cover you and all that pertains to you in the precious blood. I envelope you with the fire of the Holy Ghost. I hide you under the His protective wings. No evil will befall you. Herod will and must know that you are a big fish in Jesus' name.

Prayer Focus

- Ask the fire of the Holy Ghost to destroy every Herod that has been assigned to abort your destiny.
- Declare his plans will fail over you and your destiny
- Just as Mary and Joseph hear the word of caution from the Lord; declare that as from today you will begin to hear when God gives you a word of caution.
- Declare that the Lord will make you a terror to everything that has terrorized your life.
- Pray that God's fire will envelope you and deliver you and your family from

Reference Scripture

"Ye are of God, little children, and have overcome them: because greater is he that is in you, than he that is in the world" - I John 4:4.

2

Below are some more prophetic declarations. Speak them over and over into your life.

- ◈ God's presence will go before me.

- ◈ The power of the Almighty will sustain me.

- ◈ Heaven will support me.

- ◈ God's favor will go before me.

- ◈ The Lord shall be my helper. He will supply every need in my life according to His riches in glory.

- ◈ The Lord will make a way for me.

- ◈ God will supply help from the North, South, East, and West in Jesus' name.

- ◈ I will be the head and not tail; above and not beneath.

- ◈ God will release new helpers into my life.

- ◈ My head will not lack oil.

- ◈ My head will not be bowed.

- ◈ God will rain His rain of double blessings, double honor, double favor and double mercy upon my life and family.

- ◈ The Lord will connect me to my destiny builders, destiny helpers and destiny lifters.

- ◈ My destiny will not be aborted.

- I will experience a rain of Jubilee in my life, family, marriage and ministry.

- God will rain His rain of abundance upon me.

- He will rain His rain of deliverance upon me.

- I will be celebrated, elevated and decorated.

- I will enjoy divine presence.

- My light will shine for all to see.

- My life will not end up in disaster.

- I will not experience bitterness or sorrow.

- I will not be tired or weary. The Lord will grant me supernatural strength.

- The power of God will propel me to my place of divine fulfillment.

- I will not die before my time.

- My expectations will not be dashed.

- I will not fail on the verge of success.

- My destiny will not be hijacked by the enemy.

- I will reap the rewards of my labor and faithfulness.

- The joy of the Lord shall be my strength.

- God will grant me speed.

- I will be hand-picked for great assignments. Heaven will supply all I need to fulfill my divine assignment.

- My children will not die. They shall live to declare God's glory.

- My spouse will not die.

- God will open new doors unto me.

◈ I will break forth and break loose from every oppressing spirit.

◈ God will send me help when I need it.

◈ It is well with me in Jesus' name. AMEN!!

20

For There is Hope

"For there is hope of a tree, if it be cut down, that it will sprout again and that the tender branch thereof will not cease" Job 14:17.

Have you been cut down, trampled upon, beaten down, abused, afflicted or oppressed by the enemy? Does it look like you have fallen, never to rise up again? The Bible says in Proverbs 24:16 that the righteous man falls seven times, and he rises up again. It does not matter what the enemy has thrown at you or taken from you, you shall rise up again. It is not in God's program or agenda that you remain where you are. There is hope for you. There is hope for your destiny. There is hope for your children. There is hope for your marriage that is falling apart and for your spouse that is not born again. The devil does not have the last word over your life. He meant for you to fall, but God is saying, "You are rising up again." He meant for you to continue to circle around the same mountain. God is saying, "You are moving forward." He meant for you to be sick, God is saying, "By My stripes you are healed." He meant for you to be in darkness, God is saying, "I am the Light and there is light at the end of your tunnel." He meant for you to be alone and God is saying, "There are more with you than they which are with your adversary." He meant for it to be over for you, and God is saying, "My daughter, my son, it is not over until I say it is over!" Is there hope for the tree that has been cut down and beaten down by life, circumstances and the devil? God is saying, "As long as My life is in it, it will live again. It will surely sprout again."

> Is there hope for the tree that has been cut down and beaten down by life, circumstances and the devil? God is saying, "As long as my life is in it, it will live again. It will surely sprout again." God is making your life beautiful again. He is bringing something new from something old. He is bringing something fresh from something that has been abandoned, beaten and broken. Hope is springing up from hopelessness..........

Prayer Focus

- Command the power of the Holy Spirit to rest upon you and resuscitate everything that is dying or dead in your life.
- Ask the Holy Spirit fall upon you every day like dew from heaven.
- Declare you have a new name and a new identity. Declare you are entering a new season and a new beginning.
- Declare there will be a rising up of your finances, health and everything that is down in your life.
- Command beauty for your ashes in Jesus' name.
- Declare your life will blossom. You will be fruitful in Jesus' name.

It is the water of God, (Holy Spirit) that will cause it to sprout into a beautiful, fresh plant. God is making your life beautiful again. He is bringing something new from something old. He is bringing something fresh from something that has been abandoned, beaten and broken. Hope is springing up from hopelessness; joy from bitterness and sorrow. There is something tender and good coming out of something bruised and forgotten. Every area of your life that has been cut down will rise up again. You will rise up spiritually, physically, financially, academically, and emotionally in Jesus' name.

Just as Ezekiel spoke life to the dead bones in Ezekiel 37, God is speaking life to every dead, lifeless and stagnant thing and situation in your life in Jesus' name. Those dead bones will become an army. You will rise up spiritually and become an army the adversary will not be able to defeat in Jesus' name. The Lord is breathing His

Prayer Focus

- Pray that everything that has been cut down in your life will receive fresh life in Jesus' name.
- Pray that the Lord will give you a new name and identity.
- Pray that God's anointing and power will resuscitate your spiritual life.

breath of life upon everything that is dead in your life. They shall live again. I see your womb receiving life and carrying babies. I see the Lord reversing every negative report of doctors over your life. I see you doing what the enemy says you cannot and will not do. I see you going to high places that the enemy said you cannot attain. I speak life to that dead business. I speak life to that dead vision. I see you causing confusion in the camp of your enemies. He is causing an army to spring forth from you, in you and through you. You will not stay down. It is not your portion in Jesus' name. You will not go under. It is not your portion in Jesus' name. You will recover all in Jesus' name. God's life will birth new things in you and through you. God's Spirit will quicken your mortal body. Shall these bones live again? Yes they will in Jesus' name. Shall your eyes see good things again? Yes they will in Jesus' name. Shall your ears hear good news again? Yes, they will in Jesus' name. Shall your life ever be restored? Yes it will in Jesus' name. Shall your life experience joy and peace again? Is there hope for your destiny? Yes and yes in Jesus' mighty name!!! **AMEN** and **AMEN**!!!

Reference Scripture

"To appoint unto them that mourn in Zion, to give unto them beauty for ashes, the oil of joy for mourning, the garment of praise for the spirit of heaviness; that they might be called trees of righteousness, the planting of the LORD, that he might be glorified" – Isaiah 61:3.

21

No Restraint to Save....

"...For there is no restraint to the Lord to save by many or by a few"
(I Samuel14:6).

There is definitely no restraint when it comes to God. God can save by a million or by one. The restraint is not from Him, but from us. You may be in that ministry, church, school, community, subdivision, business, or office and you feel helpless and discouraged because things are going haywire and you do not know what to do. Do you feel lonely, helpless and overwhelmed? Do you feel you cannot do it alone and you need help? Do you feel that there is so much coming at you and against you, and the obstacles are too great? Do seem like the mountains are too high and insurmountable? The assurance we have is that God does not deal with numbers. One with God is the majority. If you put your trust in Him, He will strengthen you to do what many in their strength cannot accomplish. Your strength is in God and not in man. Jonathan knew that if God was with him he could overcome anything. He knew with God on his side, the enemies before him would be discomfited. He was sure he would have victory, and most especially, he could do anything. You are not alone. They that are for you are more than they that are against you.

> You may be in that ministry, church, school, community, subdivision, business, office and you feel helpless and discouraged because things are going haywire and you do not know what to do. Do you feel lonely, helpless and overwhelmed? Do you feel you cannot do it alone and you need help? Do you feel that there is so much coming at you and against you and the obstacles are too great? Does it seem like the mountains are too high and insurmountable? The assurance we have is that God does not deal with numbers. One with God is the majority.

As the Lord went before Jonathan in I Samuel 14, He will go before you. He will strengthen your hand to fight the good fight of faith. He will strengthen your knees to pray. He will strengthen your hands to war and

Prayer Focus

- Declare that you will accomplish what many before you were unable to accomplish.
- Ask the Lord to teach your hands to war and your fingers to fight.
- Receive grace to goforth as an arrow in the hand of a mighty man.
- Frustrate every spirit of slothfulness and complacency in your life in Jesus' name.
- Ask the Lord to flood your life with His glory and power.
- Call forth the Eagle in you to begin to soar.
- Receive grace to look up to the hills from whence your help comes and not unto man.

your fingers to fight (Psalm 144:1). Your enemies will fall before you in Jesus' name. This is your season of victory. It is your season for exploits. The people that do know their God shall be strong and do exploits" (Daniel 11:32).

If there is no constraint or restraint to God to save by many or by few, there will be no constraint or restraint with you. You will soar. You will prevail. You will avail. You will not faint. Go forth in God's power, anointing, glory and strength. Every giant that is sleeping in you will wake up and arise in the name of Jesus. I command every giant sleeping in your prayer life, in your ministry, in your home, in your mind, body, soul and spirit to arise in the mighty name of Jesus. I destroy fear and limitation. You will not be intimidated. Receive boldness and authority to go forth to conquer new territories for the Lord. Receive boldness and authority to stir those still waters. God will be glorified in your life. His joy shall be your strength. Mighty victories shall come forth through you. Your hands are anointed to prosper. Your feet are ordered by Him. There is so much He wants to do through you. What are you waiting for? You cannot afford to drag your feet. You cannot allow the devil, people, situations and circumstances to intimidate you. You cannot put your life on hold waiting for man. God is waiting for you. Please do not disappoint Him.

Prayer Focus

- Ask the Lord for the Spirit of boldness to conquer newterritories and to do those things you have not done.

Reference Scripture
"Blessed be the LORD my strength which teaches my hands to war, and my fingers to fight" - Psalm 144:1.

22

He Will Find You Out!

Jonah 1:1-17; 2:1-10; 3:1-3

Jonah was sent by God to Nineveh to proclaim doom on this great city that had done so much wickedness before the Lord. Instead of obeying God, he fled to Tarshish. He thought he could run from God's presence. How can you run from the Maker of the heavens and the Earth; the One who sees the whole universe like He sees the palms of His hand? It is impossible! Jonah was soon to learn that no matter where he hid, God was there. On his way to Tarshish, Jonah got into a ship. There arose a mighty storm that was going to destroy the ship. The passengers were so afraid everyone began to cry unto his god for deliverance. While everyone was panicking and crying to their gods, Jonah was at the bottom of the boat sleeping. When the captain of the ship found him, he wanted him to cry to his God, too, for deliverance. Jonah knew what the problem was. He knew he had disobeyed the Almighty God. When they cast lots to find out who brought this calamity on them, the lot fell on Jonah. Jonah had to confess to them that he was running from God's presence. They had no choice but to throw him overboard. The Lord prepared a fish to swallow him up. Jonah found himself in the "pit of hell" for three days and three nights! Those days were like hell to Jonah. Jonah 2:1-2 says, *"Jonah prayed unto the LORD his God out of the fish's belly, And he said, I cried by reason of mine affliction unto the LORD, and he heard me; out of the belly of hell*

> How can you run from the Maker of the heaven and the Earth.......? It is impossible! Jonah was soon to learn that no matter where he hid, God was there.

Prayer Focus

♦ Plead the blood of Jesus over your life and ask Him to forgive you for not trusting Him.

♦ If you have failed in any assignment God has given you, ask for His mercy.

♦ Ask Him to flood your life with His grace and mercy.

cried I, and thou heardest my voice." Jonah repented, cried unto God for mercy and God heard him.

Prayer Focus

♦ Ask Him to fill you with His wisdom, power, and knowledge to excel and prosper.

♦ Ask Him to lead and direct you as you go forth in doing what He asked you to do.

♦ If you are like Jonah, in the belly of a fish, ask Him to remove you from it and anoint you with fresh oil for a fresh start.

♦ Ask Him to begin to commit more into your hands and receive grace not to fail Him.

Are you like Jonah, thinking you can hide from the Lord? Are you hiding secret sins from Him? Are you delaying responding to speaking to people God has sent you to because of their position and power? Are you feeling too timid to deliver the message God has laid on your heart because you think people will not listen?

God commanded the fish to vomit him on to dry land. In Jonah 3:1-3, the Word of the Lord came unto Jonah the second time and told him to go to Nineveh and pronounce doom unto them for their wickedness and this time, Jonah arose and went to Nineveh according to the word of the Lord.

Are you like Jonah, thinking you can hide from the Lord? Are you hiding secret sins from Him? Are you delaying speaking to the people God has sent you to because of their position and power? Are you feeling too timid to deliver a message God has laid on your heart because you think people will not listen? Remember, there is no one above God; there is none bigger than Him. Has He given you salvation messages to the unsaved, and instead of preaching His messages you have decided to preach your own message of prosperity?

Are you preaching "your messages" because that is what people want to hear? Has God sent you to your family member or friend that is perishing, and you have refused to go because....?

Your assignment might just be your actions in your work place that will lead many to Christ. If you are not an ambassador of Christ in that office, family, or community, you are running and hiding from God's presence!!!

75

Jonah had to learn in the belly of a fish that no one can run or hide from God. Are you running? Are you in your pit of hell? Where are you? What lessons are you learning or have you learned? You cannot hide from His presence; but you can definitely hide in His presence. You can run into His presence today. Repent and go as the Lord has commanded you. No one is bigger than Him, not you; no one!!!

Prayer Focus

♦ Ask the Lord to draw you into His presence daily.

♦ Pray that heaven will release unto you all blessings that come from being in the presence of God.

Ask for wisdom to say all He wants you to say. Peter and John were arrested by some rulers and priests in Acts 4. They were commanded to refrain from preaching in Jesus' name. This is what they said to their captors, ".....*Whether it be right in the sight of God to hearken unto you more than unto God, judge ye.*" If it is right in the sight of God, do it! Daniel in Daniel 6 refused not go into God's presence. He would rather be thrown into the lions' den than not pray to his God for 30 days.

The Lord will help you. He will cause His anointing to rest upon you and give you boldness in the face of opposition. He will draw you back into his loving, compassionate and merciful arms. You will truly become His voice wherever you find yourself. Your actions will not cause any more people to perish. You are too valuable in the hands of God to lose. Instead of running from His presence, you will begin like never before to run into His presence for wisdom, knowledge, and understanding. You will run into it for fresh oil, and a fresh Word; not words that are diluted and watered down. If you have been discouraged, run into it for comfort. If you are helpless, run into it for help. If you are dried up spiritually and you think there is nothing left in you, run into it for a refreshing. If you do not know Him as Lord and Savior, run into it today for salvation!!! It is well with you in Jesus' name. **AMEN.**

Reference Scripture
"Thou wilt show me the path of life: in thy presence is fullness of joy; at thy right hand there are pleasures for evermore" - Psalm 16:11.

23

An Encounter with Destiny!

John 4:1-42

In this passage, Jesus was on His way to Galilee from Judea. On His journey, He passed though Samaria. According to Bible scholars, Jesus had the option of passing through two (2) other routes, but He did not. He passed through Samaria because He needed to. It was in God's program that a certain woman would have an encounter with Jesus. God knew that there was a woman who He needed a touch. He knew that there was a woman whose life had to be changed desperately forever by His presence in that city. Even though she thought all she wanted was water, Jesus knew she needed more! He knew all her life she had been going after temporal

> It did not matter what people thought about her or what she had done, in the eyes of God she was still a vessel He could clean up and use. The thing about it is that the people judging her knew her past, but did not know her future. Even though they had written her off, God by His mercy had written her in!

things and He wanted her testimony to be permanent. She had been looking unto "men" to satisfy her, but He wanted to satisfy her with something spiritual that would last her eternally. He knew that this woman who had been marred by life needed a dramatic turn around and change in her destiny so He works it out so that Jesus would pass through Samaria. Why? It was because it was the appointed time for this woman who was a 'castaway' to have an encounter with God's mercy and an encounter with destiny! It was time for her to become a

> Even though she though all she needed was water, Jesus knew she needed more. She had been looking unto "men" to satisfy her, but he wanted to satisfy her with something spiritual that would last her eternally. He knew that this woman who had been marred by life needed a dramatic turn around and change in her destiny ....It was time for her to become.......

useful tool in the hands of the Lord. She had previously had five (5) husbands and the one she was living with was not her husband! This woman who had gone through so many men was the most unlikely person anyone would listen to. However, God knew that if this woman's life was changed, many would be touched by her testimony. So, just because of her, He had to pass through Samaria! But God needed to use someone to preach the gospel and the best candidate was this Samaritan woman. She was probably ostracized and stigmatized because of what she had done. It did not matter what people thought about her or what she had done, in the eyes of God she was still a vessel He could clean up and use. The people who judged her knew her past, but they did not know her future. Even though they had written her off, God, by His mercy had written her in!

So one fateful day, while Jesus' disciples had gone into the city to get some food, she walked up to the well to fetch water and she meets Jesus alone there. A casual walk to a well becomes a walk into her destiny! When she met

Prayer Focus

♦ Ask the Lord's mercy to single you out for an encounter with the Glory.

♦ Declare that your past will not hinder your future.

♦ Declare that even though you may have started badly, God's mercy will lift you out of the miry clay and set your feet upon the Rock.

♦ Declare that your generation will celebrate your existence.

♦ Ask the Lord to give you the grace to live your life with the intention of leaving a legacy behind.

♦ Ask the Lord to order your foot steps in the pathway to your divine destiny.

♦ Pray for grace to please God all the days of your life.

Jesus, He asked her to give him water to drink. Her response to Jesus' request was, "How can you a Jew ask for water from me a Samaritan................" Jesus offered spiritual water, the water that will last through eternity. After Jesus told her some things about her life, she knew that she had met with the Christ. God could have chosen any other vessel, but He

What were the odds that Jesus was by Himself at the well on this fateful day? What were the odds that everyone who could have stopped this woman's miracle was kept at bay? What were the odds that out of all the women in that city, this marred Samaritan woman was the one that was chosen?

chose one that was not perfect; one that had been marred by life.

What were the odds that Jesus was by Himself at the well on this fateful day? What were the odds that everyone who could have stopped this woman's miracle was kept at bay? What were the odds that out of all the women in that city, this "unqualified" Samaritan woman was the one chosen? The only answer to the question is God's mercy. God's mercy enabled her to encounter the Glory, Jesus! His mercy singled her out! When God's mercy opens a door, no one can shut it! God's mercy is available to single you out too!

Prayer Focus

- Frustrate every plan of the enemy to prevent your encounter with God's glory.
- Declare your life will not be in vain.
- Declare you will end well.
- Declare God's mercy will provoke His glory in your life.
- Declare God's mercy will cover your weaknesses and open the door into your destiny.

It was God's mercy that singled out Moses and caused him to encounter God's glory. It was as a result of this encounter that a man who was slow to speak was able to lead 600,000 Israelites out of Egypt to the promise land. It was God's mercy that singled out Rahab the harlot and made her part of the lineage of our Lord Jesus Christ. It was God's mercy that picked Ruth, a Moabitess and made her the great grandmother of David the king. It was God's mercy that picked out an unlearned fisher man called Peter and made him preach a message that brought 3,000 souls to the Lord (Acts 2:41). It was God's mercy that picked out Saul of Tarsus, a persecutor of the Church and turned him into an Apostle who wrote about two-thirds of the New Testament (Acts 9). And the list goes on and on. It is God's mercy that will pick you too out for His glory!

God used this woman to preach to the men of the city that had used and abandoned her! God's hand will rest upon you to do the unimaginable in Jesus' name. The Lord will use you for people who have mocked and despised you. The stone which the builders have rejected will now become the corner stone (Psalm 118:22; Matthew 21:42). God's power will cleanse you. His blood will wash you. His mercy will prevail over your life. Your destiny will not be aborted. You will become a wonder. God will use you for His glory. He will heal your body, soul and spirit. God's glory will surround you in Jesus' name. **AMEN.**

Reference Scripture

"But God hath chosen the foolish things of the world to confound the wise; and God hath chosen the weak things of the world to confound the things which are mighty and base things of the world, and things which are despised, hath God chosen...." - I Corinthians 1:27-28.

24

Send My "Simon", O Lord!

Mark 15:1-21

There are certain things we cannot do except there is an intervention from an outside source or power. There are doors we cannot open except God opens those doors. There are places we cannot go except God goes before us. There are mountains we cannot move unless God moves them for us. There are mountains we cannot climb unless God supplies the strength and help. In other words, we need divine help to do anything outstanding in life. We need God's help to fulfill our destinies. God can send man. He can send angels. He can send the Holy Ghost. He can use living and non-living things when He is ready to bless you. He can send help in your darkest hour. Are you in need of God's help? This is your season of divine assistance in Jesus' name

> There are certain things we cannot do except there is an intervention from an outside source or power. There are doors we cannot open except God opens those doors. There are places we cannot go except God goes before us. There are mountains we cannot move unless God moves them for us. There are mountains we cannot climb unless God suppliesthe strength and help. In other words, we need divine help to do anything outstanding in life.

God will also use your friends and enemies. He will use strangers. He will use people who hate you for no just cause to get you to your "Golgotha". He used Judas, Pilate, the Pharisees and Sadducees, and even the soldiers to get Jesus there! Each person, good or bad had a role to play and each person's role was in God's divine agenda so that the scripture might be accomplished! Judas' kiss of death was in God's divine plan. In Mark 15, Pilate delivered Jesus into the hands of the soldiers to be crucified even after he was sure that Jesus was falsely accused. The soldiers scourged, beat and spat on Him. They put a crown of thorns on His head, mocked and humiliated Him. They put the weight of the cross upon Him to carry to Golgotha where He was to be crucified. Unknowingly to them, they were helping Jesus fulfill the purpose for which He came to the world. Golgotha represented His "promised land."

All the wrong they did to Him was leading Him to the place of the fulfillment of His purpose here on Earth. Even though the cup was bitter, He drank it anyway. Don't fret when people you have done no wrong hate you. Their purpose in your life is to lead you to your divine purpose.

On the way to Golgotha, they saw a man named Simon, who was compelled to help Jesus carry the cross to the place where He was to be crucified. I am certain Jesus must have been physically tired from the continuous beating and humiliation. He did not fight back, but continued to carry the cross until God sent help. In your most difficult moment in life, when it appears all hope is lost and there seems to be no way out, God will bring your "Simon" and use him/her or it to help you carry your cross, ease your pain, pay your debt, bring a word of comfort, lift your burden and bring you to the place of the fulfillment of your destiny.

At Golgotha, Jesus recovered all. You too will recover all in Jesus' name. Nothing will stop you from reaching your goal. Nothing will stop you from fulfilling your destiny. Nothing will stop you from doing all that God wants you to do on this side of eternity. You will reach your promised land. Your "Simon" will emerge. No power from the pit

Prayer Focus

♦ Pray for supernatural strength and courage in the face of adversity.

♦ Declare that your helpers will come from the North, South, East and West in Jesus' name.

♦ Just as Jesus received help from His enemies, pray that God will cause your enemies to help you reach your goal and divine purpose.

♦ Just as Jesus received help from Simon, a stranger; pray that help will come from people who know you and people who do not know you.

♦ Declare that God's power will blow upon you the wind of His divine help.

♦ Declare that all that you are going through and all that you have gone through will lead you to the fulfillment of your divine purpose.

♦ Begin to declare and decree that noticeable and undeniable testimonies will begin to happen in your life.

♦ Declare all you have suffered and labored for in your life will not be in vain.

♦ Declare you will end well in the mighty name of Jesus.

Prayer Focus

♦ Pray that the mark of God's favor will be upon you and open the eyes of your helpers to see you.

♦ Pray that the heavens over your life will open and release all the help that you need to fulfill God's divine purpose for your life..

♦ Declare strangers will build your walls.

♦ Declare all God's creation will work in your favor to help you reach your goal and divine purpose.

of hell will stop you from attaining your goal. Your "Simon" will lose his/her sleep just because of you. Your "Simon" will not die until they fulfill God's purpose in your life. There is a bright shining light at the end of your tunnel. You will not die before your time. God replaced Jesus' shame with glory and honor. Your shame will turn to honor. Your rags will turn to riches; your sickness to health in Jesus' name. It is my prayer that God's power will remove everything standing between you and your destiny. Just as nothing was able to stop Jesus from getting to His place of divine fulfillment, nothing will stop you. As you cry out to the Lord, He will send your "Simon" in ministry. He will send your "Simon" to your home. He will send your "Simon" to your business. He will send your "Simon" in every area of need in Jesus' name. God will usher you into your season of divine fulfillment. He will cause you to enjoy rest. Every stormy situation will receive God's peace. You will not stumble or fall on the way. You will go from strength to strength and from glory to glory. The Holy Spirit will empower you. He will send help from the North, South, East and West. He will strengthen and uphold you. Your hope will not be shattered. You will not be weary. Your strength, joy, honor and glory will be restored in Jesus' name.

Reference Scripture
"God is our refuge and strength, a very present help in trouble.Therefore will not we fear, though the earth be removed, and though the mountains be carried into the midst of the sea" - Psalm 46:1-2.

25

A New Thing!

Acts 19:1-7

In the above mentioned passage, Paul came to Ephesus and met twelve disciples there. He asked them if they had received the Holy Ghost since they believed. They said they had never heard of the Holy Ghost. They had only experienced John's baptism, which was the Baptism of Repentance. But that day, they heard a new thing; something they had not heard before. They heard that there was another baptism, the baptism of the Holy Ghost. After Paul laid hands on them, they had a new experience. They were baptized with power! They had experiences before, but nothing like this one!

> Do you believe God for new experiences? Do you want to replace the old with the new? Do you want God to take you to another level? Do you want to see and hear what others have not seen or heard? Do you want the Lord to open your life to new experiences?

Can you believe God for new experiences? Do you want to replace the old with the new? Do you want God to take you to a new level in Him? Do you want to see what others have not seen or hear what others have not heard? The Lord is saying that this season as you seek Him more, He will take you to a new level. Do you want the Lord to open your life to new things? He will open your ears to hear new things. He will open your eyes to see new things. He will open your ministry to experience a new dimension of His power and glory. Your

> I wondered why they did not have this new encounter before Paul's visit to Ephesus. John the Baptist had been with them. Apollos had also been with them. They both taught the same thing. I do not know how many other apostles or disciples had visited Ephesus before Paul. But why now? Why not through the others?

Prayer Focus

- Thank God for the word He just ministered to you.
- Ask Him to empty you and fill you afresh with new oil.
- Pray that the Lord will cause you to pant and yearn for more of Him.
- Declare that the Lord will open your life up to new experiences.
- Pray that the Lord will make you a bearer of the good news people want to hear.
- Pray that the power of the Holy Ghost will remove any obstacle holding you back from experiencing all He has for you.
- Declare the each day you live on the face of the Earth will be better for you than the day before it.
- Declare that God's presence will be real in your life every day of your life.
- Declare that God will find you faithful and select you for heavenly assignments.

marriage will experience new wine. You will experience a new wave of His glory and power.

He is saying it does not matter what you have experienced before now; you will experience more. It does not matter what level of anointing you had before now; you will experience a new anointing. It does not matter who is ahead of you; He will cause you to overtake. He will use you for things people before you are coveting. He will take you to places people before you have not been. You will begin to hear what you have not heard before in your life in the mighty name of Jesus.

Ps 42:1 says, *"As the deer pants after the waters so my soul pants after you, O God."* Take time to seek His face. Keep asking for more. Do not give up. I don't know at what level you are spiritually, the Lord is saying that you have not yet reached your climax. In II Kings 2, just as a double portion of the spirit that was on Elijah rested on Elisha, the Lord will give you double for your trouble. In the same passage, Elisha ripped off the old to pick up the new. The power of the Lord will remove everything that may stop the new from being manifested in your life and family. He will do a new thing in you, for you and through you. You will become a conduit of God's power and glory. You will become a bearer of the good news people want to hear in Jesus' name.

Perhaps you have not heard any good news in a while; you will hear your good news in Jesus' name. Maybe you have not seen anything spectacular lately; you will see and manifest it in Jesus' name. Do you feel like you are marking time and looks like you are

Prayer Focus

♦ Pray that God's mark of favor will be upon you so that your blessings will not elude you.

♦ Many destinies have been aborted because of wrong timing; pray that your destiny will not be aborted. You will be favored by God and man.

♦ Pray that by the mercy of God, you will not miss your season.

♦ Pray that the Lord will open a book of remembrance and your name will be found in it.

♦ Pray that every day of your life you will have spectacular experiences that will mark a turning point in your life.

♦ Pray that the Lord will remove the old and engulf you with the new.

♦ Pray that you will daily have a craving and a yearning for more of God's power, anointing, presence, holiness and righteousness.

♦ Pray that God's fire will burn off the old and put upon you the new.

going nowhere? You will move forward. You will break forth. You will break through in Jesus' name.

God told the Israelites in Deuteronomy 1:6 that they had dwelt long enough on the same mountain and He commanded them to go in and possess the land which He swore to their fathers. You will go forward. You will possess your land. You will see and experience new things in Jesus' name. God's glory will envelope you. You will experience His favor.

I cannot but wonder why these twelve disciples were the first ones to receive the baptism of the Holy Ghost under Paul's ministry in Ephesus. I also wondered why they did not have this new encounter before Paul's visit to Ephesus. John the Baptist had been with them. Apollos had also been with them. They both taught the same thing. I do not know how many other apostles or disciples had visited Ephesus before Paul. But why now? Why not through the others? It was their time to experience something different. Acts 19:1 says that Paul found these twelve disciples. The Lord will find you. When it is time for you to experience His divine visitation, you will not be found missing. Your steps will be divinely ordered by the Spirit of the Lord. The Lord will anoint your feet to walk into new doors. He will anoint your hands to receive new things. He will favor you. He will set you apart. He will single you out for a new thing. He will open doors of

Prayer Focus

♦ Pray that your fire will be contagious and others will have their new experiences from your encounter.

♦ Pray that the anointing to be a soul winner will rest upon you.

opportunities for you. Doors that have been shut against you will begin to open in Jesus' name. The Lord will open doors to a new chapter and phase in your life, family and ministry. He will equip you for great works. He will equip you with all you need to fulfill your destiny. You will be relevant. Heaven will remember you. You will see and experience what others in your extended family have not seen or experienced. You will experience a new beginning. You will not be stagnant. You will go from strength to strength and from glory to glory. The Lord will take you to a new level in Him. He will take you to a new level in ministry. He will take your ideas to a new level. He will take your vision to a new level. He will take your marriage and relationship to a new level. He will take your finances to a new level. He will take your health to a new level. He will take your business and career to a new level. He will baptize you afresh with His Spirit. You will experience a new anointing in the mighty name of Jesus. **AMEN**.

Reference Scripture
"Eye has not seen, nor ear heard, nor have entered into the heart of man the things which God has prepared for those who love Him"- I Corinthians 2:9.

26

God Will Surely Honor You!

Acts 28:1-10

n Acts, 27, Paul and 275 other people had just gone through a grievous storm and escaped from a ship wreck. The angel of the Lord had told Paul that no one would perish from the storm. Paul had to step in and put the minds of all the travelers at ease. So according to Paul's word, they all got to the island of Malta safely. After they had all arrived on the island safely, I am almost certain that Paul and the people with him must have been rejoicing because they had all just escaped death. I can just imagine how happy they must have felt after they got over the near death experience. In Verse 2, the natives on the Island received them and showed them kindness. I believe Paul was in a good place; at least he had a few days to rest from all the troubles he had just been through. Unfortunately, his so called rest was short-lived! As he was gathering sticks to put in the fire, a viper came out of the fire and fastened itself on his hand. Why Paul? Why not somebody else? Why not one of the 275 passengers that were with him? Why not one of the people from the island? Why did this have to happen to the one God had just used to get them all to safety? Why did this happen when everyone must have been looking

Prayer Focus

- Pray that God will disappoint every evil plan of the adversary over your life and family.
- Pray that God's hand will rest upon you for double honor.
- Declare your shame will turn to honor.
- Pray the Lord will celebrate you everywhere you have been despised.
- Declare that the plans of the enemy to disgrace you will be aborted in Jesus' name.
- Plead the blood of Jesus upon yourself and family and pray that the blood will defend you from destruction and calamity.

Prayer Focus

♦ Pray that your present state will not abort your future.

♦ Declare that you will begin to receive honor from those that do not know you.

Prayer Focus

♦ Ask the Lord to vindicate you in the presence of your mockers and accusers.

♦ Declare honor will come from those who have despised you and put you to shame.

♦ Declare that the storms in your life will become the vessels to propel you to your destiny.

♦ Declare that your mourning will turn into dancing.

♦ Declare that your enemy will not rejoice over you.

Prayer Focus

♦ Pray your victory will be permanent.

♦ Declare every plan to abort your joy will be destroyed.

♦ Declare that the Lord will reverse every negative situation in your life.

at him as their hero? Lord, why now? Why did this have to happen when he was supposed to be rejoicing over a victory? Why this setback?

When the people saw that the viper had fastened itself on Paul's hand, they immediately concluded that he was a murderer and that his evil ways were catching up with him; that is why out of over 200 people he was the only one attacked by this venomous beast! It is very typical for people to quickly make their judgments and switch sides, loyalty and allegiance when you have a setback; what some call, "hosanna today, crucify tomorrow." The same people he saved from a wreck are now calling him a murderer. However, Paul immediately shook the beast into the fire. The people from the Island stood watching expecting him to swell from the poison and drop dead, but it did not happen! The enemy's plan and plot over your life will not prosper in Jesus' name. After a while when nothing happened to Paul, they changed their minds about him and said that he was a god!

The story did not end there. Publius, one of the leading citizens of the Island invited them to his house and entertained them for three (3) days. While in his house, Publius' father fell sick. God used Paul again. He laid his hands on Publius' father and healed him. When others from this island saw what happened, they began to bring others with diverse sicknesses to Paul and he healed them all. In Verse 10, because of Paul, all the prisoners with him were honored by the natives. When they were leaving, they blessed them with all they needed. What a blessing! This was the same person that was in a shipwreck, bitten by a poisonous snake and called a murderer. God turned shame and reproach into a season of honor for Paul. Are you asking questions and wondering why you are facing so many challenges now? Does it look like when you have overcome a storm or challenge, another one rears up its head and it feels like an unending vicious cycle? Have you been unfairly accused of something you know nothing about? Have you been called negative names by people who know you and some who know nothing about you? Are you in a position that if God does not do something quickly, the end result will be shame? Have you suffered reproach and shame from the hands of people who should honor you?

> Are you asking questions and wondering why you are facing so many challenges? Does it look like when you have overcome a storm or challenge, another one rears up its head and it feels like an unending vicious cycle? Have you been unfairly accused of something you know nothing about? Have you been called negative names by people who know you and some who know nothing about you? Are you in a position that if God does not do something quickly, the end result will be shame? Imagine God bestowing honor on a prisoner!

Have you been calling on God and asking Him to honor Himself in the midst of the challenges you are facing? Are people looking on to you for answers, which you do not have? Have you been passed over? It is time for God to honor you no matter your situation or condition. Imagine God bestowing honor on a prisoner! God is not a respecter of persons. If he did it for Paul, He can do it for you. In the midst of Paul's dilemma, God blessed him and made him a blessing to many. In the midst of his storm, God showed up and showed out. In the midst of adversity God showcased him. God disappointed the evil craftiness of the enemy and caused him to prevail.

It is the same God declaring and conferring His honor upon you this season. No matter what you have faced or are facing, God's honor will speak for you. God will re-write your destiny. A new page of a new chapter of honor has been opened for you by the power of the Holy Ghost. He will give you a name change. He will transform your destiny. He will remove your shame and you will become a blessing to those who have written you off. The hand of the Lord will lift you up. The glory of the Lord will shield you. His honor will announce you. Everything that the enemy has programmed to kill you will be reversed in Jesus' name. The Lord will turn your mourning into dancing. Instead of death, I speak life to you. Instead of shame and reproach, I speak honor and glory. God will turn every plan of the enemy to humiliate you into honor. The Lord will disappoint those waiting for you to fall. They will wait in vain in Jesus' name. It is well with you in the mighty and precious name of Jesus. **AMEN.**

Reference Scripture

"Instead of your shame you shall have double honor, and instead of confusion they shall rejoice in their portion. Therefore in their land they shall possess double;Everlasting joy shall be theirs" - Isaiah 61:7.

27

Just Come!

Matthew 14:22-33

Jesus sent His disciples into a ship and asked them to cross over to the other side while He went up to the mountain to pray. When the ship got to the middle of the sea, there arose a great storm that tossed the ship back and forth. You might ask,"Did Jesus not know that there was going to be a great storm that could wipe out all His disciples? Why would He send them across the sea if it was going to become a dangerous adventure? Why did the storm begin when they had reached the middle of the sea where there was no turning back, and no one to help them?" Jesus knew what was going to happen. He is an all knowing God. He is the Answer to every question! He knows all about the questions you are asking Him today. "Why Lord?" In the midst of the chaos, Jesus started walking on the water towards His disciples. Imagine Jesus walking on the same sea that was experiencing the storm!!! When the disciples saw Him, they could not believe their eyes when He announced Himself to them. As Jesus announced Himself to the disciples that day, He is announcing Himself to you. He is announcing Himself to your situation and circumstance.He is the One that calms the raging storm, the Alpha and Omega. He is

> Did Jesus not know that there was going to be a great storm that could wipe out all His disciples? Why would He send them across the sea if it was going to become a dangerous adventure? Why did the storm begin when they had reached the middle of the sea where there was no turning back, and no one to help them? Then Jesus announced Himself to them. As He announced Himself to the disciples that day, He is announcing Himself to you. He is announcing Himself to your situation and circumstance. He is the One that calms the raging storm, the Alpha and Omega, the on-time God, never too late, the Helper of the helpless.

the on-time God. He is never late. He is the Helper of the helpless! He is the Bridge over stormy waters. He is your Deliverer.

It does not matter what storm you are going through today: It may seem your ship is about to capsize or fall apart, He is announcing Himself to you. When Peter realized that it was Jesus, he asked if he could come over and Jesus told him to come. Just as Jesus said to Peter, "Come," He is saying to you, "Come, it does not matter the condition of your ship. Come, it does not matter what is happening in your home. Come, it does not matter what is happening in your body. Come, it does not matter what is happening in your finances, mind, marriage, business, ministry, or church. Just come!!!"

Peter heeded to Jesus' call and he began to walk on the water in the midst of the storm. Can you do the unimaginable or the unexpected if God calls? There were other disciples in the boat, but only Peter asked if he could come. Only Peter ventured to walk on the water in the midst of the storm. Only Peter asked. God is looking for pacesetters in the kingdom. Can He trust you to be the one? He is looking for people who will step out of their boat into the storm to overcome it. Even though Peter became afraid in the middle of His storm, Jesus was there to take Him up and rescue Him from it. Are you bold enough to step out against all odds and do what God has been calling you to do?

Prayer Focus

♦ Ask the Lord open your ears to hear Him when He is calling.

♦ Ask Him to anoint your eyes to see Him in the midst of your storm.

♦ Ask the Lord for strength to do the unimaginable in your workplace, business, and ministry.

♦ Receive boldness in the face of adversity, shame and reproach.

♦ Pray that God's power will uphold you so that you will not suffer a shipwreck spiritually.

♦ Ask for grace to heed to the voice of the Lord so that you can become a trailblazer in your generation.

♦ Ask Him to give you the grace to step out against all odds.

♦ Pray that you will not be put to shame.

♦ Pray for the anointing of an overcomer.

The storm started in the midst of their journey. Are you experiencing delays, attacks and setbacks in the middle of an assignment or project? Are you experiencing a setback in the prime of your life? Are you experiencing continous setbacks that you feel are out of the ordinary and it feels you are experiencing a viscious cycle? Do you feel alone and it seems you are sinking? Does it look like if God does not take you up and save you today, you will end up in destruction and embarrassment? You will not be destoyed in Jesus' name. You will not die before your time. I prophecy God's Spirit of boldness upon you. I frustrate the spirit of fear. In the name of Jesus. I frustrate and come against every storm that has tossed your life and destiny back and forth. I break the hold of every negative cycle in your life today in the mighty name of Jesus. I command every foundational storm to cease now in the name above every other name, the name of Jesus the Son of the Living God. I speak the peace of God upon you right now in Jesus' name. I speak God's peace into your life and situation. What the enemy meant for evil, I turn it around for your good in Jesus' name. I speak against the root cause of everything that has tormented you and has not allowed you to step out into God's calling and purpose for your life.

If Jesus had not held out His hand to rescue Peter, Peter would have either drowned or he would probably have become a laughing stock among the other disciples. God's mighty hand will rescue you from destruction and embarrassment. You will not perish. You will not be put to shame. You will walk over your storm and overcome it in Jesus' name. God will reverse situations and circumstances the enemy meant to embarrass you. Nothing will stop you from reaching your goal. God will give you peace in the midst of it. You will walk over the fear tormenting your life. Just as Peter was the first in his time to walk on water, you will become a pacesetter in your generation; the first to do strange things. God will make you a positive point of reference to many. In verse 33, those that were in the boat who witnessed this miracle worshipped Jesus. Many in the same boat as you will witness your transformation and worship your God in the mighty and precious name of Jesus. **AMEN.**

Reference Scripture

"Do not be anxious about anything, but in everything by prayer and supplication with thanksgiving let your requests be made known to God. And the peace of God, which surpasses all understanding, will guardyour hearts and your minds in Christ Jesus" - Philippians 4:6-7.

28

Set Up My Stage!

II Kings 8:1-6

In the above mentioned passage, the Shunammite woman left to go to the land of the Philistines for seven years at the word of Prophet Elisha. When she came back, she discovered that she had lost all her possessions. So she went to the king's palace to cry for help and beg that her possessions be restored to her. In the meantime, Gehazi, Elisha's servant was at the king's palace having a conversation with the king. The king wanted to know all the great things that Elisha the prophet had done. Can you imagine the miracle Gehazi decided to share with the king? It was about that of a woman whose son was raised from the dead by Elisha. He happened to be sharing the testimony of the Shunammite woman! As Gehazi was speaking to the king about her and her son, she and her son walked into the king's palace! Just imagine how Gehazi must have felt when he saw her walk through the door. It was apparent that the king did not know this woman because Gehazi had to introduce her to him. He said, "This is the woman, my lord the king, and this is her son whom Elisha restored to life." The testimony was right before them! The miracle could not be denied! Immediately, the king assigned an official to her case and said they should give her back everything that belonged to her, including all the income from her land from the day she left the country.

Prayer Focus

- Pray that God will send your "voice" of deliverance, restoration and lifting before you every day of your life.

- Pray that God's favor will go before you wherever you go.

- Declare that your miracle will come effortlessly in Jesus' name.

- Command the power of God to remove every hindrance in the way of your blessings.

- Pray that God will divinely order your steps to your divine destiny.

- Pray you will enjoy the fruit of your labor

Are you looking unto God for help? Have you been crying and it does not seem like anyone is listening? Have you been denied what rightfully belongs to you? Are you looking unto God for your "voice" in the midst of chaos? Have you been cheated and it seems everything you have tried to do to get your stuff back has failed? Have you fought so long and are now tired of fighting? Have you resolved in your heart that if any help will come, it will only come if and only if God raises "voices" on your behalf?

Prayer Focus

♦ Pray that people who know you will favor you; people who do not know you will favor you.

♦ Pray that heaven will raise help for you anytime you need it.

♦ Declare God's anointing for grace, mercy, provision and abundance will rest upon you.

♦ Pray that God will set a stage for your miracles.

It was nothing but God's hand upon this woman. He sent a "voice" before her to speak on her behalf. She did not have to spend long unending hours wailing and pleading before the king to get what rightfully belonged to her. God had sent the "voice" to do it for her! The voice of her lifting, recovery and restoration had gone ahead of her. The Lord had set a stage for her miracle!

Are you looking unto God for help? Have you been crying and it does not seem like anyone is listening? Heaven will respond to your cry in Jesus' name. Have you been denied what rightfully belongs to you? Are you looking unto God for your "voice" in the midst of chaos? Have you been cheated and it seems everything you have tried to do to get your stuff back has failed? Have you fought so long and are now tired of fighting? Have you resolved in your heart that if any help will come, it will only come if and only if God raises "voices" on your behalf? May your "voice" never be silent until they do all that the Lord wants them to do in your life, home, ministry and business. Just as the Lord set a stage for this woman's miracle, He will set a stage in every season of your life and present your miracles to you on a platter of gold. The "voice" that you need to take you to your destiny will fight day and night for you. Your destiny helper will not die on the verge of your breakthrough and success. The voice of your destiny helpers will not be drowned by the enemy. God will raise help for you in the time of need. Your heavenly voices will speak. Angels will be at attention just because of you. God the Father, Son and Holy Ghost will favor you. The

Trinity will help you. Jesus your Mediator will fight for you. He will defend you. You will not be frustrated. You will not be abandoned. You will not be put to shame.

Prayer Focus

♦ Pray that your voice of lifting and breakthrough will not be drowned in the midst of chaos.

♦ Declare that help will arise every time you need it.

The king did not know this woman, but he favored her all the same. Those who do not know you will help you. The Lord will order your footsteps. You will not run full speed in the wrong direction. Your miracle will not be delayed. Your healing will not be delayed. Your deliverance will come when you need it. You will be in the right place at the right time. Heaven will fight for you. Before you call God will answer you and show you great and mighty things. You will recover all that you have lost. You will recover your joy. You will recover your peace. You will recover your home. You will not die on the verge of your breakthrough. You will recover your business. God will redeem your time. The Lord will encourage you with testimonies that will cause the ears of your detractors to tingle. Your testimony will encourage others. God will put a new song in your mouth in Jesus' name. **AMEN.**

Reference Scripture

"Do not be anxious about anything, but in everything by prayer and supplication with thanksgiving let your requests be made known to God. And the peace of God, which surpasses all understanding, will guardyour hearts and your minds in Christ Jesus" - Philippians 4:6-7.

29

Hope in Your Valley

Ezekiel 37:1-10

Ezekiel was taken in the spirit to a valley that was full of dry bones. The Bible says the bones in this valley were very dry. The Lord asked him, *"Can these bones live?"* And Ezekiel answered God, *"Thou knowest."* Ezekiel knew it could only take an act of God for these very dry bones to come alive. So God said to him, "Prophesy to the bones..." God assured Ezekiel that He will:

- Cause breath to come upon them and they will live
- Lay sinews (tendons) upon them
- Bring flesh upon them
- Cover them with skin
- Put breath in them
- And they shall live

Prayer Focus

♦ Pray that God's power will bring to life everything that is dead, dormant or stagnant in your life.

♦ Command God's fire to go to your foundation and cause a revival in your life.

♦ Pray that the four winds of the Earth will blow your blessings to you in Jesus' name.

What an awesome Word of power and encouragement to bones that had definitely been forgotten in this valley! So Ezekiel did as the Lord commanded him. He prophesied and after he did, there was a noise and a shaking. There was commotion. Each bone looking for its match! The bones came together bone to bone and sinews (tendons) and flesh came upon them and skin covered them. The Lord was not done. He told Ezekiel to prophesy to the four winds to breathe upon the slain that they may live. And he did. As he did, breath came upon them and they came alive and stood up on their feet, an exceeding great army. What a testimony!

Prayer Focus

♦ Pray that God's glory will cover your shame.

♦ Declare that the power of the Holy Ghost will make you a positive point of reference.

♦ Pray that God's power will shake and rebuild your foundation.

The Lord did everything He said He would do to the dry bones. Even though men had forgotten about them, God did not. Even though men thought it was over for them, God knew there was hope in this abandoned valley. He knew there was life in this dead place. Looking at the valley with the natural or human eye, it did not look like anything could come out of it. It was impossible for a miracle like this to come out of such a miserable place; but it did! These very dry bones had destiny in them. They were not destined to die forever. They were not destined to be forgotten forever. Even though the flesh on the bones was decayed, there was still something fresh, new and beautiful coming out of them. Their glory was not meant to be covered. They had to live! In the beginning it did not look like a miracle could come from this dead valley, but it did.

God's Word and Spirit came into the valley and caused it to live again. It is the same thing that happened in Genesis 1. Just as God spoke to the Earth that was void and without form and caused life to spring out of it, God told Ezekiel to speak to the valley of dead bones and life came out of it. Also in Psalm 23, David said, *"Even though I walk through the valley of shadow of death, I will fear no evil for Thou art with me Thy rod and Thy staff they comfort me......"* And the Lord is saying to you. "Even though you are in the midst of your valley, believe that there is a miracle in it because I am with you. Believe there is hope in the valley. I am not done with you yet! It does not matter how it looks or what people have said about you or your situation, I am not finished with you. I will cause everything that is dead in your valley to come alive and live. I will cause the miracle in your valley to come out." God is saying to you, "Speak, prophesy to your valley; there is a miracle in it. Speak to that sickness in your body. Prophesy healing to your physical body. Command all dead cells to come alive" He wants the champion in you to arise. He wants the light in you to shine. He wants you to arise and shine for your light has come and the glory of the Lord shall rise upon you (Isaiah 60:1). He wants your glory and destiny that have been buried and hidden to come up and show forth. He wants His power to cause a shaking in the foundation of your life and destiny and shake loose everything that has held you bound. Your chains and fetters will be broken. Your yokes will be destroyed. God's power will set you free in Jesus' name.

Are you dead or dying spiritually? God wants to revive you. I speak life to that lukewarm spirit in the name of Jesus. I speak to that spirit of slumber and say, "Arise in Jesus' name." God wants to revive your spiritual life. He is saying, "There is still a miracle of salvation and redemption in your valley. There is a miracle of salvation in your home." God wants to breathe upon you and cause you to come alive. He does not want to touch just you; He wants to touch your family. He wants it to begin with you. He wants you to begin to touch others. He wants your life to become a testimony in the mouths of those that know you.

Are you nursing a dead business or dead marriage? God wants to resuscitate it. Is a dream that the Lord gave you dying or is it on life support? Don't give up. Speak to it. It may not look like it, but there is hope in your valley. There is a miracle in your valley. Just because the bones in it are dead or seem dead, it does not mean they are useless.

You must believe in the Resurrection and Life. You must believe in the One who has the power over death. Are you ready? If so, release yourself. Yield yourself to Him and call forth those dead bones in the name of Jesus. I join my faith with yours today and together we prophesy life upon you. We declare that God's fire will come upon you. We prophesy a revival in your bones. You will live for Him. Your life will testify to the goodness of the Lord. We prophesy life to your home and marriage. Your home, marriage, children, business and everything about you will testify to the goodness of the Lord. Everything that is scattered or out of joint will come together in your life. God will cover your nakedness. He will beautify your life. He will restore your hope. He will restore your foundation. Everything in your foundation that needs a touch from heaven will receive it. He will empower you and anoint you with the anointing of a champion. He will anoint you with fresh oil and your cup will run over. Those things that have defeated you or prevailed against you in the past will become a stepping stone for you into your victory. Your shame will turn to honor. There is hope in your valley. Your valley of dry bones will live again in Jesus' name. **AMEN.**

Reference Scripture
"'The glory of this latter temple shall be greater than the former,' says the Lord of hosts. 'And in this place I will give peace,' says the Lord of hosts" – Haggai 2:9.

30

Indeed You are Barren, But You Shall Bear

Judges 13:1-3

The above mentioned passage talks about God's divine plan for His people, the Israelites, even though they had sinned against Him. It also talks about His divine plan to use a barren woman to be the vessel to produce the deliverer of His people. The Bible does not tell us what qualified this woman for this great blessing or what caused her to be visited by what I call an "Angel of Hope;" an "Angel of Good Tidings." I call it GRACE, unmerited favor!!! God's grace rested on this woman and singled her out. He gave her not only what she desperately needed, but what a whole nation needed! Her prayers were answered, and at the same time her "gift" became an answer to the prayers and cry of a nation. Although she had been tagged "Barren," she would give birth to a son that would deliver Israel from the hands of the Philistines. In verse 3, the angel said, "Indeed now, you are....but...." God is saying, "This is your reality now, but it is not my final plan for your life. This is the doctors' report, but that is not my TRUTH for you. This is what people have labeled you, but it is not what I am calling you. This is what man sees, but it is not what I see in you and for you. This is where you are right now, but it is not your final destination!!!" You have had great challenges, and you may be having greater challenges but my word for you is, "Even though you walk through the valley of the shadow of death, whatever challenges that you are facing now, I am with

Prayer Focus

- Declare that your reality will be replaced by God's Truth.
- Declare that the blood of Jesus will remove every negative mark in your life in Jesus' name.
- Ask that God's presence will overshadow you and deliver you from every valley of shadow of death you are facing.
- Pray for the greatness within you to break forth.

The Bible does not tell us what qualified this woman for this great blessing or what caused her to be visited by what I call an "Angel of Hope;" an "Angel of Good Tidings." It is GRACE. God's grace rested on this woman and singled her out to give her, not only what shewas in dare need of, but what a whole nation needed! Her prayers wereanswered and at thesame time, she became an answer to prayers.

you." God is saying, "There is greatness in you. You are pregnant with life. Destiny has to be birthed through you. Your latter end must and will be more glorious than your former. It is not over for you yet. I am re-writing your story. Your story will be a point of reference for many lives. My grace is upon you to change every negative report and turn your destiny around!! Your miracle will not just be yours alone, you will be an answer to the prayers of many. You will no longer be judged by your past."

God's grace and mercy will prevail over your life and give you a new beginning. You will no longer be spiritually blind; the eyes of your understanding will be opened. He will give you the mouth and the ears of the learned. You will no longer be in spiritual darkness. God's light will illuminate your way. You will no longer be spiritually barren. You will know the Truth and you will cause many to know it too!! You will no longer be physically barren; you will conceive and bear children. Your quiver shall be full. Do not think or try to figure out how God will do this. He will turn every negative report of the doctors around in your favor!!!

God said to the woman, "Thou shall conceive and bear a son, but thou shall not......." The Lord is saying to you, "If I promise to make you fruitful and erase

Prayer Focus

♦ Ask that your "Angel of Hope" will visit you and turn every hopeless situation in your life around.

♦ Ask that the Lord will make your gift an answer to your generation.

♦ Bless God for what He has done.

♦ Give Him glory, honor and adoration.

and eradicate every form of barrenness from your life, you shall no longer do what you have been doing. You can no longer remain where you are today in your walk with me. You will have to move forward for the past will no longer haunt you. You must be obedient to me and do as I tell you. It is a new season and a new dawn in your life. There are things that you can longer do, relationships you can no longer keep. I will have to become your Source, Your Love and Your God. Now that you have become a carrier of My glory, your body has become My temple. I have decided to invade your life and use you for My glory! An anointing for fruitfulness shall rest upon you and you shall not lack peace, honor, grace, favor, anointing, wisdom and understanding." He is saying, "Just do as I say. Read and obey my Word and it shall be well with you. Your children are blessed. Your business is blessed. Your finances are blessed. Your ministry is blessed. Whatever you lack today, you will lack no more. Follow the blueprints of my Word."

Make the following declarations:

I turn around every negative report that has been pronounced over my life into testimonies. God will put His hand afresh upon me. I declare that my testimony will become a blessing to generations after me. I will birth destiny. I am a carrier of God's glory. I am fruitful spiritually and physically. I am fruitful in every area of my life. God's Spirit will water my waste places. I will not be put to shame. It is a new day; a new season. I am bursting forth into my morning.

There are many who will be reading this book that will conceive. You may have been called barren and waiting on the Lord for years for the fruit of the womb; the power of God will open your womb, open every blocked tube and every organ will begin to work in alignment to God's divine purpose. Life will flourish in your body. There will be no more miscarriages in Jesus' name. Your business will flourish. Your children will flourish. Your ministry will flourish. Your home will experience joy and peace it has never experienced. You are marked to be used for God's glory in Jesus' name. **AMEN.**

Scripture Reference
"....I will take away sickness from the midst of you. None shall suffer miscarriage or be barren in your land; I will fulfill the number of your day." - Exodus 23:25-26

3

Finally, here are some more blessings. Declare them over your life and destiny and it shall be well with you.

- ◈ I rebuke every devourer in my life and family.

- ◈ The Lord will remove every mountain and Goliath in the path of my destiny.

- ◈ The fire of the Holy Ghost will rest upon me and cause me to move to a new level supernaturally.

- ◈ The Lord will grant me the Spirit of Wisdom, Knowledge, Understanding, the Spirit of Counsel, Might and the Fear of Lord.

- ◈ I am contagiously blessed.

- ◈ The Lord will give me the tongue of the learned.

- ◈ I will not mourn or sorrow over my children.

- ◈ I will become relevant where I have been despised.

- ◈ I will not beg; I will not be put to shame.

- ◈ God's glory will cover me and beautify my life.

- ◈ An end has come to failure in my life; success is my portion.

- ◈ My life will not be aborted. I will not die before my time. I will enjoy long life.

- ◈ The devil will not have the last word over my destiny.

- The Lord will anoint me daily with fresh oil.

- Each day I wake up will be better than the day before.

- I will enjoy fresh revelation every day.

- I will ride upon my high places. I will ride on the wings of the Eagle.

- The Lord will bring water out of my rock and honey out of my carcass.

- I will rule, reign and have dominion over the kingdom of darkness.

- The Lord will hold me by the hand and lead me by His strength and power. I will not miss my divine appointment.

- I will not fail. I will not fall and I will not be defeated.

- God's fire will surround me and protect me from all evil. Every oppression will cease in my life.

- My life will be meaningful and it will add value to others.

- I will no longer be despised. I will no longer be scorned. God's glory will announce me wherever I go. I have become a carrier of God's glory and honor.

- The fragrance of God's favor will rest upon me.

- The Earth will cooperate with my destiny.

- When others are saying there is no way, I will have at least seven options.

- The last defeat I encountered will be the last I will ever encounter.

- I am more than a conqueror.

- God's goodness and mercy shall follow me every day of my life and I will dwell in the house of the Lord forever in Jesus' name. AMEN.

Whose Guest Will You Be At the End?

Everyone who dies will rise up at the end, no matter the lifestyle they lived. Death is a gate. When it comes, calling each of us will be received by one of two hosts; God or Satan. Those who are welcomed by Jesus will sit with Him at the right hand of God the Father (I Peter 3:22). Revelation 14:13 says that they will rest from their labor for their works will follow them. However, for those who are welcomed by Satan, it means their names are not written in the book of life. Revelation 20:15 (NIV) says, "Anyone whose name is not found in the book is thrown into the lake of fire." For both of them death is not the end. It is the beginning of a new life; either with Jesus in heaven or with the devil in hell. No one knows when the end will be. Whenever it is, now or later, whose guest do you want to be?

If you have not accepted Jesus Christ as your Lord and Savior, the only way to attract God's blessings and the blessings in this book is to give your life to Him. You can tell Him to come into your heart today and transform it. It is not about Church attendance, singing in the choir, being on the Usher Board or how long you've been a member of your church: It is about asking Him into your life and cultivating a relationship with Him. This decision will be the first "Defining Experience" of your life and the most important decision you'll ever make.

You must believe that: Jesus is the Son of God; He died for your sins (Romans 10:9); He was raised from the dead; and He lives forever more. You must acknowledge, repent, confess and forsake your sins (Luke 13:3, Acts 3:19, I John 1:9, Isaiah 55:7) and ask Him for forgiveness (Romans 3:23, 6:23). Tell Him you want to begin to live for Him and not for yourself. Ask Him to replace the old man with His Spirit. Ask Him to write your name in the Lamb's book of life. Ask Him to lead you every day in your new walk. Thank Him for coming into your life. Now, if you have just received Jesus into your life, I want to congratulate you and welcome you into the Body of Christ. Finally, being a Christian is not about works. The work of the cross was done for you. However, to grow and mature in your new walk, you need to do the following:

- Pray every day
- Read the Word every day
- Join a life-giving, bible-based Church where you can grow and fellowship with other believers
- Make disciples. Share your testimony with others so they too can join you and have the same experience you just had. God Bless you!

You can now turn the pages over to the beginning of this book and begin to enjoy all God's blessings in His Word and in every chapter of this book. Peace and Joy to you!

HELP IN THE TIME OF NEED

◆ **ABOUT FORGIVEMESS:**
Matthew 6:14-15; I john 1:9; Isaiah 43:25-26; Acts 3:19; Isaiah 1:18; II Corinthians 5:17; Ephesians 1:7; Colossians 1:13-14; Mark 11:25.

◆ **ABOUT FAITH:**
Matthew 21:21; Hebrews 11:1; I Peter 1:21; II Corinthians 5:7; I Corinthians 15:4-7; I John 5:4; I Corinthians 16:13: I Peter 5:9; I Corinthians 2:5; Ephesians 2:8; Ephesians 6:16; Galatians 3:11-12; Galatians 5:5; John 14:12; Hebrews 12:2; Romans 10:17.

◆ **FOR MARRIAGE:**
Isaiah 3:10; Proverbs 31:10-29; Psalm 1:3; Psalm 128; Ephesians 5:22-23; Psalm 68:6.

◆ **WHEN LONELY:**
Deuteronomy 31:6; Psalm 23; Psalm 27; Hebrews 13:5; Matthew 28: 20.

◆ **FOR SUCCESS ON EXAMINATIONS**:
Genesis 39:1-5; Psalm 119:34-125; Psalm 71:1-7; Daniel 1: 10; Ecclesiastes 7:11-12.

◆ **FOR PROMOTION:**
Psalm 75:6-7; Psalm 8: 7.

◆ **FOR HEALING:**
Psalm 107:19-21; Exodus 23:25-26; Isaiah 53:4-5; Psalm 103:2-4; Psalm 41:2-3; Jeremiah 17:14; I Peter 2:24.

◆ **BEFORE TRAVELLING:**
Psalm 121; Psalm 128; Psalm 91; Isaiah 54:17.

◆ **BEFORE STARTING A BUSINESS:**
Genesis 39:1-5; Psalm 1:3; Psalm 90:16-17; Job 14:7; Deuteronomy 28:7-8, 11.

◈ WHEN IN LACK:
Job 36:11; Psalm 34:10; Matthew 6:33; Philippians 4:15; III John 2; John 14:14; Isaiah 41:18.

◈ FOR PEACE:
Psalm 55:22; Matthew 11:28-30; John 14:27; John 16:33; Philippians 4:6-7; Psalm 3:5-6; Jeremiah 29:11; Isaiah 40:29-31; Philippians 4:19; Proverbs 1:33;John 14:27.

◈ FOR STRENGTH:
Psalm 119:28; Ephesians 6:10; II Corinthians 12:9-10; Psalm 46:1-11; Isaiah 40:28-31; Isaiah 41:10; Isaiah 12:2; Exodus 15:2; Psalm 18:32-34; Ephesians 3:16; Psalm 28:7-8; Psalm 118:14; I Corinthians 10:13; Deuteronomy 31:6; Psalm 23:4.

◈ FOR HOPE IN THE MIDST OF CRISIS:
Psalm 27:4-5; Mark 5:35-36; Numbers 23:19; Zephaniah 3:17; John 4:13-14.

◈ FOR THE PREGNANT:
I Timothy 1:4; Exodus 23:26; Malachi 3:11 Matthew 4:10 Isaiah 66:7-8; Joshua 2:4-6; Deuteronomy 28:1-14; Job 5:26; Deuteronomy 712-15; Isaiah 65:23.

OTHER ARTICLES

STEWARDSHIP

I Corinthians 4:1

A stewardin the Bible is someone who has the responsibility to manage all that God has entrusted to him or her. Good stewardship is the proper management of all that God has trusted into our care. A steward goes by many titles: a servant, manager, chief servant or servant-in-charge. Whatever the title, he is God's manager of resources that He put in his or her charge. God has called us all to be stewards of one thing or the other. We are stewards in the church, stewards in our homes, stewards in the work place, stewards in the marketplace, stewards of our money, stewards of our time, stewards of all He has given to us and made available to us.

What kind of steward are you? Does your service or management help to promote the purposes of God or promote yourself? A good steward recognizes the following:

- **He or she belongs to the Lord**. This is exactly what Paul says in *Romans 1:6 when he reminds Christians that they "belong to Jesus Christ."*

- **That everything he has belongs to the Lord.** Joseph is a prime example of a steward as Genesis 39:4-6 records, "Potiphar put him [Joseph] in charge of his household, and he entrusted to his care everything he owned. From the time he put him in charge of his household and of all that he owned…So he left in Joseph's care everything he had. "He or she knows that God is the owner of everything and that we are the servants and managers of what He has entrusted into our hands.

In I Chronicles 29 11-14, after David purchased and gathered all the materials with which to build the temple, he prayed and praised God for all He gave him and dedicated all to Him. In his prayer of dedication, he praised God saying, *"Blessed are You, Lord God of Israel, our Father, forever and ever. Yours, O Lord, is the greatness, The power and the glory, The victory and the majesty; For all that is in heaven and in earth is Yours; Yours is the kingdom, O Lord, And You are exalted as head over all. Both riches and honor come from You, and You reign over all. In Your hand is power and might; in Your hand it is to make great and to give strength to all. Now therefore, our God, We thank You and praise Your glorious name. But who am I, and who are my people, that we should be able to*

112

offer so willingly as this? For all things come from You, and of Your own we have given You."

- **That all he enjoys belongs to God and is a gift to him not only for enjoyment, but for service**. Practically, this means the air we breathe, the food we eat, and everything else is a gracious gift from our loving God. Stewards seek to faithfully oversee all that God has entrusted to their oversight. Because they see that they and all that has been entrusted to their care belong to God alone, they aspire to manage everything in their life in a God-glorifying way. Additionally, they do not want to be guilty of robbing God by failing to manage his resources according to His will.

- **That God put him in charge of all the things He created.** The Steward's real job is faithfulness. God has clear instructions for stewards. "Now it is required that those who have been given a trust (literally, stewards) must prove faithful" (1 Corinthians 4:2). Psalm 8:6 says. "You have made him (man) to have dominion over the works of Your hands; You have put all things under his feet."

A steward has been entrusted with gifts for service to God and others. Good stewards manage their time to use the gifts as God intended. A faithful steward cares for his body because he recognizes that his body is a temple of the Holy Ghost (I Corinthians 3:16-19; 6:19). A steward has been entrusted with the management of money and possessions. Many of Jesus' parables dealt with money and possessions. The gift of money and possessions have been given to us for a purpose; and the purpose must glorify the Giver. A good steward gives offering, sows seeds and pays his tithe. . Tithing is a form of returning one-tenth back to God (Genesis 14:20; Genesis 28:22; Malachi 3:6-12). Jesus affirms the practice in Matthew 23:23; Luke 11:42 and Apostle Paul teaches it as proportionate giving (I Corinthians 16:1-2).

A steward has been given the secrets to the kingdom. The secrets are in the Good News (Bible) that leads to salvation and life in Christ. He must study, believe and receive the word. He must also live and proclaim the words in the Good News to the unsaved, not only through their words, but by the way they live. A good steward is an example to the saved and unsaved. He must know that the unsaved prefer to live their own lives rather than live according to the teachings of the Bible. He must know that he is held accountable for all he says and does. He is held accountable for how faithful he is.

Jesus talked about good and bad stewards (Matthew 25:14-30; Luke 12:42-48). Good stewards not only take care of what God has given them, but multiply its value. In the parable in the book of Matthew, the steward that was given five talents multiplied it by two. He bought back ten talents. The steward that was given two (2) talents also multiplied it by two and brought back four (4). But the one that was given one talent only buried it for safekeeping.. The master was very displeased with him. He took his talent from him and gave it to the one that had ten talents. Are you burying your talent? Are you being safe? Being a good steward is more about revolution than evolution. We can't change our world if we are not being the salt of the earth. A Christian should enhance the environment around him/her.

Finally brethren, God wants us to be good stewards so that on the day of reckoning we will be rewarded for our good works.

UNITY

When the world talks about unity, I believe they are simply referring to tolerance. The worldly concept of "tolerance" emphasizes the acceptance of our differences, while the Bible emphasizes a more deeply rooted and profound concept. For example, tolerance says that it accepts all things and people, but does not carry along with it the implicit biblical requirement to love and embrace unconditionally: It merely suggests a superficial acquiescence to the political, social and cultural ways of our society and, right or wrong, allows for different ways of thinking and behaving to become the norm. Christianity, on the other hand, says that, though others might be different and even wrong about something, they can still be loved. Tolerance doesn't love others enough to tell them that they are wrong, unless of course they are being "intolerant." If tolerance is practiced in the church, then truth will be minimized, love will be exchanged for acceptance, and true Biblical unity will be forfeited. (Romans 12:2-3)

John 17:21-23 says, "That they may all be one; even as You, Father, are in Me and I in You, that they also may be in Us, so that the world may believe that You sent Me. The glory which You have given Me I have given to them, that they may be one, just as We are one; I in them and You in Me, that they may be perfected in unity, so that the world may know that You sent Me, and loved them, even as You have loved Me."

There is, however, unlimited power in unity! Unity simply means having continuity in purpose or action. Psalm 133:1 says, "Behold, how good and how pleasant it is for brethren to dwell together in unity!"(NKJV). Unity is the glue in the body of Christ that allows us to be one in spite of all our differences: different perspectives, races, experiences, and denominations. There is nothing the devil fears more than Christians who are united. This means that his number one tactic is to bring division in the Church. If he can succeed, then the Church is crippled.

Jesus spoke about the power of agreement in Matthew 18:19: "Again, I tell you that if two of you on earth agree about anything you ask for, it will be done for you by my Father in heaven." As a Church, we can receive anything if we agree about it in prayer. The Bible in Deuteronomy 32:30 says that one can put a thousand to flight, but two could put ten thousand to flight. Together we can accomplish more than when we work alone. In Genesis 11, the people in Babylonia began to work together, and they accomplished an enormous feat—the building of the tower of Babel. Although their hearts were wrong, they were at least unified. And what did God say concerning the power of their unity?

He said, "Nothing they plan to do will be impossible for them!" God knows the power of unity. Unity will work for the unsaved like it will work for saints. This is exactly why the unbelievers have made such advances, while the church is trying to keep up.

The three key components associated with unity are **agreement**, **harmony** and **oneness**. But to be in agreement, harmony and oneness, we must truly love one another.

- **AGREEMENT**–*"Again I say unto you, that if two of you shall agree on earth as touching anything that they ask, it will be done for them of My Father in heaven. For where two or three are gathered together in My name, I am there in the midst of them"* -Matthew 18:19-20 (KJV). At the core of unity is the principle of agreement. Unified agreement in the body of Christ brings answers to our prayers, fulfillment of our needs and the very presence of the Holy Spirit into our midst. In Acts 2, the 120 disciples in the upper room were united and their unity invoked the presence of the Holy Spirit. Where there is the Holy Spirit, there is power. Signs and wonders followed the ministry of the apostles because there was unity in the early Church. If we agree, there can be harmony. We are stronger together than separate. The Bible says that one will put one thousand to flight, but two will put *ten thousand to flight* (Leviticus 26:8; Deuteronomy 32:30).

- **HARMONY** – It is the combination of simultaneously sounded musical notes to produce chords and chord progressions with a pleasing effect. Everyone loves to hear a symphony play with harmony by blending separate, individual sounds to create one sound. This is what we can do in the body of Christ to more effectively influence the world in which we live. Paul spoke of harmony in Galatians 3:28, *"We are no longer Jews or Greeks or slaves or free men or even merely men or women, but we are all the same--we are Christians; we are one in Christ Jesus."* (Living Bible). Paul also said in Romans 14:19, "So then, let us aim for harmony in the church and try to build each other up."

- **ONENESS** (one heart and one mind) – Jesus set an example by having oneness with the Father. He prayed in John 17:11, *"Holy Father, I am no longer in the world. I am coming to you, but my followers are still in the world. So keep them safe by the power of the name that you have given me. Then they will be one with each other, just as you and I are one."* (Contemporary English Version) Together, we can make a Kingdom impact that will leave an indelible impression upon a generation yearning for the validation of its significance and purpose.

Purposes of the Church are:

- To worship God
- To build up the saints
- To spread the Good News

Just as Jesus said to his disciples, "Your love for one another will prove to the world that you are my disciples." (John 13:35), so is unity important for accomplishing all three purposes of the Church.

Pre-requisites for Unity:
- Being content toward self - "Walk worthy of the vocation wherewith you were called" (Ephesians 6:1). When you are content with yourself or love yourself, there will be no jealousy or envy.
- Being content toward our fellow man – "With all lowliness and meekness, with long-suffering, forbearing one another in love"(Ephesians 4:2). When we are content with each other, we will truly love each other.
- Being content toward God – "You must love the Lord your God with all your heart, all your soul, and all your mind. This is the first and greatest commandment (Matthew 22:37-38). When we are content with God, we will love Him above everything.

It's time that we stop the division and strife in the Body of Christ. It is time to strive for unity. When we do, we will become a mighty force in the kingdom, accomplish a lot for God and put the devil to shame. When we are united, we will accomplish more. Where there is disunity and strife, the devil is able to take over and do havoc, but when there is unity among brethren, there is strength. Drops of water are very little things, but when they are collected, they make the vast ocean. Grains of sand are also very little things. But the vast land is made of them. Each blade of grass is not a strong thing but when a rope is made of them, an elephant can be bound. An ant cannot drag a dead insect or a bit of food but when many ants try together, they can drag it easily.

The enemy has come to steal, kill and destroy (John 10:10). One of the ways he can accomplish his purpose is through disunity among brethren. God is looking for those that will stand up against all that the enemy is doing against the Church and say, "It is time to put a stop to his antics. We are ready to put our differences aside and do all God has called us to do."

PROCRASTINATION

Matthew 25:14-30

The above mentioned passage recounts Jesus' parable of a man who was on his way to a far country. He called three (3) of his servants and gave then five, two and one talent respectively. He gave then the talents according to each man's ability. The one who received the five talents traded with it and gained five extra talents. The one who was given two also traded with it and gained two extra talents. The one that was given one talent dug a hole and buried his master's talent in there. After a long time, the lord of the servants came back. The one who had received the five talents brought five other talents and delivered them to the lord. The one who received the two talents also brought the two talents he had gained and delivered them to the lord. And the lord said to each of the servants, 'Well done, good and faithful servant; you have been faithful over a few things, I will make you ruler over many things. Enter into the joy of your lord.'

However, the servant who had received the one talent came to him with excuses and said, 'Lord, I knew you to be a hard man, reaping where you have not sown, and gathering where you have not scattered seed....I was afraid, and went and hid your talent in the ground. Look, there you have what is yours." The lord said to him, 'You wicked and lazy servant, you knew that I reap where I have not sown, and gather where I have not scattered seed...... take the talent from him, and give it to him who has ten talents. For to everyone who has, more will be given, and he will have abundance; but from him who does not have, even what he has will be taken away.........." What a tragedy!

The Lord is talking to us in this passage about the following:

- Procrastination (delaying a course of action) – This is one of the greatest enemies of success. The servants given the two and five talents did what they had to do diligently before the lord came back so they could get the reward they deserved. Isaiah 1:19 says, "If you are willing and obedient, you shall eat the good of the land." The procrastinator did nothing, but hid the talent until the lord cane back. The Lord does not want us as His children to put away or hide any assignment, gift, talent that He has given us. If he gave it, He expects us to use it.

- Faithfulness – If you are faithful in little, the Lord will commit greater things into your hands. It was sad that the servant that hid his talent lost it to one of the other two servants. Jealously guard your gift. It is yours to use for God's glory. He will reward your faithfulness in Jesus' name.

- Opportunity – Each servant was given the opportunity to prove themselves. Two passed and one failed. You will not fail God, yourself, your children and your generation in Jesus' name.

- Wisdom – The two servants that did what their lord asked them to do were wise. Wisdom is the application of God's word.

- Decision-making - All three had the opportunity to make a decision. To go forward or to mark time; to increase or to be stagnant. Some decisions are hard and difficult, but the end result is gain. The Lord will give you the grace and back you up as you make the difficult decisions that you have to make this year. You will not be put to shame in Jesus' name.

- Promotion – Each servant was one-move away from their promotion. Each one was one move away from their destiny. It is that move in board game "Checkers" that is referred to as the "check mate."

- Favor – Each servant had an opportunity to enjoy favor from the lord. Every step that you take according to God's will and in obedience to His word will earn you favor. God will reward your obedience with favor and advancement in Jesus' name.

- Business – It teaches us to do business in a way that will glorify God. We have to be good stewards of our time, talents and treasure or otherwise they can be taken away and given to another.

- Completion – We must learn to complete whatever we start. Starting and not completing tasks is a sign of procrastination and slothfulness. The lord gave the three servants same tasks; only two of them completed their tasks. There is no way God can commit anything into the hands of a procrastinator or someone that is slothful.

- Respect – Respect is not demanded. It is earned. You do not have to tell anyone who is boss. All you need to do is lead and people will follow.

- Perception – How you see things determines how you act. Because the two servants had a perception of respect and honor for the lord, they obeyed him. The one servant who hid his talent had a perception of disrespect and dishonor which showed in his words and actions. He disobeyed, made excuses and insulted the lord. The first two had promotion and blessings. The lord said ".....I will make your ruler over many things (promotion), enter into your rest (blessing)." If we do not honor God and perceive Him right, we will go about doing what we want to do and expect God to bless it.

- Take responsibility – Everything that happens to us is not the fault of the enemy. We have to take responsibility for our actions.

PROCRASTINATION (PART 2)

Matthew 25:14-30

<u>Signs of a Procrastinator</u>

Every negative thing that happens in our lives is not the devil's fault. All of us at one point have put off doing things. Below are some tell-tale signs:

1. Do you delay until it is too late to start a project?
2. Do you collect materials for projects but struggle to get started?
3. Do you obstruct the efforts of others by delaying doing your part?
4. Do you deliberately work slowly and inefficiently?
5. Do you resent suggestions on how to work more productively?
6. Do you avoid competition in situations where you might not succeed?
7. Do you act indecisively and force others to make decisions?
8. Do you avoid responsibility by making others feel guilty?
9. Do you avoid making commitments?
10. Do you become irritable when asked to do something unpleasant?
11. Do you find yourself consistently late for appointments, then get mad when they charge you?
12. Do you ever avoid obligations by choosing to forget them?
13. Do you pay your bills and other financial obligations late consistently then get mad when you get a reminder phone call?
14. Do you live in a constant state of disorganization?
15. Do you become addicted with time wasting activities such as watching television, talking on the phone, texting, skyping, etc.?
16. Do you feel spiritually bankrupt, yet fail to appropriate God's promises in His word?
17. Do you lack accountability from God for failing to heed conviction from Him?
18. Do you desperately need direction, but have no time for God?

If you have answered yes to some or all of these questions, you need to ask for grace to do better.

How Can I Overcome Procrastination?

Here are a few tips:

1. Make *change* your friend. Change has to be viewed as a blessing and not a curse. Change may cause pain. However, the pain is temporary. Change will always cause discomfort. Most people quit because of the pain. It will cause you to walk by yourself. Even though Change takes us to unfamiliar territory, the end result is great.
2. Divorce negative self-talk. Divorce the "What ifs?" and "how can?" What ifs an how cans keep you in a constant state of negative influx. You are the greatest prophet over your life. It is not what anybody says about you that matters, it is what you say about yourself that matters most. Begin to think positively and to speak positively.
3. Do not put off till tomorrow what you can do today. Get a grip and just do it. At the end, it boils down to taking action. You can do all the strategizing and planning, but if you don't take action, nothing's going to happen. Reality check: I have never heard anyone procrastinate their way to success. If you want to get it done whatever it is you are procrastinating on, you need to get a grip on yourself and do it.
4. Manage your time. Avoid time wasters. You may have to reassess some relationships. Hang out with people who inspire you to action. Identify the people/friends/colleagues that trigger you: These folks are most likely the go-getters and hard workers. Hang out with them more often. Soon you will inculcate their drive and spirit.
5. Develop a hunger for self-improvement. The only two (2) feet you can control are the ones you stand on. No one can rob you of the value you have in investing in yourself. What investment are you willing to make in yourself this year? What do you want to do with the time you have left? What would you put in place if you had a week, a month, six months or a year to live? What would you put in place in your life today that will make 2014 the beginning of the greatest years of your life?
6. Anytime you make a change, there will be resistance; resistance from yourself and others. Once you put your mind to do something, do it. Don't look for excuses and reasons why it will not work. Persistently pursue your dreams.
7. Guard your mind. Do not listen to the excuses of the enemy. Do not reason with him. If he can control your mind, he can control your actions. He controls your

mind if he can get you to think the wrong things, believe the wrong things or do the wrong things.

8. Follow the vision in front of you. Develop an action plan and stick to it. Ask the Lord to lead you. Ask Him for strength to continue in that path.

9. Follow the plan of God. Doubt is the first step toward failure and defeat because it affects every choice you make.

10. Seek out someone who has already achieved the outcome. What is it you want to accomplish here, and who are the people who have accomplished this already? Go seek them out and connect with them. Seeing living proof that your goals are very well achievable if you take action is one of the best triggers for action.

11. Don't let your emotions dictate your actions. How you see (perceive) things determine how you act.

As you take a bold step to disappoint procrastination today, the Lord will make you prosper in all that you do. The devil will not disappoint your actions. Your life will be fruitful. The Lord will crown your year with great success. You will end the year well in Jesus' name. Your testimony will be, "thou good and faithful servant, enter into your rest."

About the Author

Pastor Bola Adepoju, is the founder of Woman on Purpose. She is an advent speaker with an unusual calling to women of all ages, races and ethnic background. She is a preacher, a conference speaker, an exhorter, a motivational speaker and a prophetic intercessor, with an unusual insight into the Word of God. She is a Fellow of the Black Women in Ministerial Leadership Fellowship. Her love for the unsaved, afflicted and oppressed has taken her overseas as she fulfills her mission and call to transform lives, heal hearts and win souls. Hers is a message of the 21st Century; a message for the voiceless, boldly declaring a message of hope, truth, and wholeness; compelling the attention of those seeking to discover their purpose in life; those seeking to launch into their destiny and those seeking to know God more. Her motto in life is: "There is nothing God cannot do. With God on your side, there is nothing you cannot do. The only person that can stop you is you."

She has to her credit several published and unpublished articles. She is the author of the book titled, "Woman on Purpose." Published in 2009 as "Mujer a Propósito", the Spanish translation is gaining grounds in the Hispanic community. Her bi-weekly newsletter titled, "Woman on Purpose" is transmitted to women in various parts of the U.S. and the world. Her newsletters have been compiled into a series of books titled, "Inspirations".

Pastor Bola received her Bachelors of Arts degree at Spelman College and her Masters in Business Administration from Atlanta University, both in Atlanta. She is married to the love of her life and is blessed with two beautiful children.

Other Books
By
Bola Adepoju

WOMAN ON
PURPOSE
By Bola Adepoju

MUJER A
PROPÓSITO
Bola Adepoju

ISBN 978-1-4257-5480-8

Mujer a Propósito
ISBN: pasta blanda 978-0-9762681-0-9

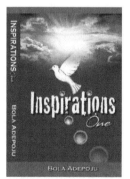

Inspirations I
ISBN 978-0-9891977-0-0

Paper Back & E- Books
Available at
www.womanonpurpose.org
& at your on-line stores

To Contact Pastor Bola Adepoju, please write to:

Woman on Purpose

P.O. Box 2910

Stockbridge, Ga.30281

or

visit: www.womanonpurpose.org

or

e-mail: pastorbola@womanonpurpose.org

42228041R00079

Made in the USA
Charleston, SC
23 May 2015